Harry

Barnsley

working as a child labourer and served his ... the RAF during the Second World War. Afterwards he returned to civilian life by marrying and, along with many from his generation, helping to lay the cornerstones of the welfare by becoming an engaged citizen.

At ninety-four, Harry is an activist for the poor, the NHS and the preservation of social democracy. He is the author of five books and a frequent contributor to the *New Statesman*, *Daily Mirror* and *Guardian*, for whom his video essay on the refugee crisis was shared over a million times on Facebook and has attracted huge comment and debate. Refusing to go gently into that good night, Harry now hosts a weekly podcast. When not on the road speaking about his life experiences, he divides his time between Yorkshire and Ontario, Canada.

Don't Let My Past Be Your Future

Harry Leslie Smith

CONSTABLE

CONSTABLE

First published in Great Britain in 2017 by Constable
This paperback edition published in 2018

1 3 5 7 9 10 8 6 4 2

A CIP catalogue record for this book
is available from the British Library.

ISBN: 978-1-47212-347-3

Typeset in Sabon by SX Composing DTP, Rayleigh, Essex
Printed and bound in Great Britain by Clays Ltd, Elcograf S.p.A.

Papers used by Constable are from well-managed forests
and other responsible sources.

Constable
An imprint of
Little, Brown Book Group
Carmelite House
50 Victoria Embankment
London EC4Y 0DZ

An Hachette UK Company
www.hachette.co.uk

www.littlebrown.co.uk

*For my grandchildren Matthew and David
as well as their generation who must fight
against the dying of the light*

Contents

'we that are young
Shall never see so much, nor live so long.'

The Duke of Albany in *King Lear*

Prologue

In the fading light of an English summer sun, on a quiet beach located on our southern coast, I watched the tide break upon the shore and surge back towards the deep. Its roar drew me to the water's edge where I cooled my bare feet, like I had done in 1927 when I visited the sea for the first time. Then, I was a bairn of just four on a bank-holiday outing to Southport with my parents and older sister Alberta.

It was the first and last vacation I would have with my parents because, two years later, the crash of 1929 destroyed Britain. It ruined us along with millions of other families who were caught in the violent buckling of the world's financial tectonic plates that reduced Britain's working class to beggary.

Above me, a lonely gull rode slips of air and mournfully screeched out across the empty ether as if calling for absent friends, lovers and mates. I understood the bird's melancholy because in the wind I heard death whisper that he was coming for me.

My life is at eventide, and the curtain of night is closing in upon my time on this earth. I am almost one hundred years old. I know death is waiting for me but there are still some things that I must do before my life's journey is complete. I must set before my grandchildren and others the story of my early life. I must let them know about my struggles and that of my generation to build a more equal country for all and how that relates to today's politics. I must remind them to be vigilant against demagogues because the ugly spectre of fascism has started to stir again across the globe. It was contained once behind the thick walls of a functioning welfare state but, as they have now begun to crumble, all past evils are running out like mice through rotting floorboards. There is so much I must say because I do not wish to suffer the torment my mother endured before she died. She had kept her tongue still about many regrets in her life.

Ah, poor Mum, her guilt was great – it was bigger than the cancerous tumour killing her – for sins she thought she'd done to my dad, me and her other children during the Great Depression era. She begged for my forgiveness, for the harm she may have caused me during the 1930s. 'I was trying to keep thee alive and thy sister but it was so bloody hard.'

Whether it's summer or winter, my body is always cold now. I can feel, in my bones, that same chill I felt as a lad when the icy winds came down off the Yorkshire Moors in late autumn. During those days when winter was at our windowsill, my mum would lament, 'Fetch some coal for your mam, and I'll light a fire that will warm our blood. I'll tell you tales of your ancestors, who lived in Yorkshire for as long as there has been history written about our land.'

Now, at the age of ninety-four, I know death is coming for me and there are not many more winters, springs, summers or autumns left for me to see. Each season that now passes is a reminder that it may be the last time I bask in the glow of sunshine, feel the sting of an autumn rain or sense the cold when snow falls upon my face.

Even when I go to sleep, I feel death is waiting for me: I see his visage in the corner of my dreams. He beguiles me in slumber because I often see the dead faces of my parents, my sisters, brothers, wife and my middle son beckoning me to follow them.

Ah, death didn't have as much patience for those I loved as he has had with me. No, he took my sisters, my wife and one of my sons too soon. It was as if he was in a rush and needed to satisfy quickly his appetite for their lives.

When death comes for me I will walk with a calm certitude into his jaws. I'll go willingly to the other side because I've fought death many times. In fact, I've been battling and cheating death since my birth in the slums of Barnsley, where infant mortality was as deadly as it is for kids in many Third World countries today. I've been outrunning death from the moment the midwife slapped my bottom with hands calloused from scrubbing stone floors and rolling coarse shag cigarettes between her fingers.

Death didn't catch me when I was a child because I was too nimble. However, in the 1920s and the 1930s, he didn't have to run far to steal another child's life because systemic poverty had left millions of bairns in Britain susceptible to all manner of diseases or illness. Poverty and societal indifference could make one's time on this earth a brief, fleeting appearance if you were from the working class.

Hell, I even beat death in the maelstrom of the Second World War when over 60 million lives were extinguished across the continents of this earth. Death came for all of those victims of war as if those individuals were no more than flames on Captain Webb matchsticks being blown out on a draughty street. Snap and the lives of millions were extinguished. It's hard to believe, but I walked away from the greatest letting of blood known to civilisation without even a shaving nick when all of Europe was reduced to a charnel house because of the mad ambitions of dictators and demagogues. Today, when I see the politics of hate erupt up like diseased ooze from an infected boil across nations that once held firm to democracy, I cannot help but think of those long-dead tyrants such as Hitler, Stalin and Tojo who set the world of my youth ablaze.

Still, I survived those days and when I exchanged my RAF blue serge uniform for a worker's smock and cap, after the war, I survived life in the civilian world. But it was easier to live after the war because the world was changing and a new ethos was developing that proclaimed everyone had a right to a good life regardless of where they stood on society's ladder.

Prologue

Somehow, death didn't have as much determination to finish me off back then as he does now. He approaches me with a resolve to have done with me. This time, I am sure death won't let me slip through his snare like he has too often over the years that we have been acquainted. Now, he stalks me in the same manner as a lion hunts wounded prey with a slow ease because it knows that it can snatch me at any moment.

Still, he has an appetite for me. I feel him waiting for me in the shadows like a mugger waits in a ginnel for drunks after last orders.

After so many years alive, I am comprised of many moments that are both ordinary and profound. They define my personality and my outlook on life. But they will all evaporate from me like smoke from a chimney pot on a winter's morning when the second of my two remaining sons closes my eyes on my death bed and my body is dispatched to the crematorium ovens. My ashes will be scattered over the dales of Yorkshire that I once rambled across with my young wife and our friends during a time when Britain was transforming itself into a social democracy after the Second World War.

Once my mortal remains have been dissolved by the hard rains that frequently fall upon Yorkshire, I am confident that my sojourn on this earth, my few good deeds and my many human trespasses will be quickly forgotten by all but a handful who knew me. Within a year or less of my death, even their memories of all my character traits – the way I combed my hair, laughed, drank my coffee, acted decently to one person or perhaps failed to empathise with another – will evaporate like rain in the desert.

Sometimes I wish humans could live as long as the Galapagos Islands turtle so we might acquire some wisdom. But I am not so sure we would any more after so many senior citizens voted for Brexit or Donald Trump. Perhaps it's the young today that have wisdom because they are learning to live with the selfishness of the baby-boomer generation that helped create neo-liberalism and made it fashionable to disparage the welfare state while enjoying all of its benefits.

The span of my life leaves me in awe. To think, I was born only twenty years after Kitty Hawk when humanity first took to the skies in primitive mechanised flight in 1903, and now nuclear missiles can reach their targets thousands of miles away in less than thirty minutes. Our thirst to do great things like find a cure for cancer and our hunger to do harm to others like selling weapons to Saudi Arabia astonish me.

Make no mistake; I know we have progressed much since I was in short pants. When I was born, your class determined the quality of your life. But after the war against Hitler, the notion that wealth entitled you to the best of times, and poverty the worst, was done away with; the welfare state and improved education helped make Britain a meritocracy. Alas, the price of a long life is perhaps to see the axis of society gravitate back to the past.

Prologue

Housing and education are again increasingly becoming something only the rich can afford. In 2017, a house costs on average seven times the annual wage of the purchaser. Owning a home is out of reach for many, who can't even rely upon affordable housing since around eighty councils have no social housing thanks to right-to-buy; for those who live in areas that still have social housing, waiting times can be a decade or more. This has caused the use of private rental accommodation to increase by 50 per cent since 2002 and, as demand is high, rents have become precipitous.

The situation has been no different when it comes to higher education ever since the Tories, from the 2012 academic year onwards, trebled the cap for undergraduate tuition fees to £9,000 per annum. As the government has also axed grants for poor students, it is little wonder that only 32 per cent of respondents in a 2016 survey conducted by the Institute for Higher Learning said they were getting value for money. Today's young know what my generation learned a long time ago: the future is precarious for those who live on the periphery. It staggers me to think that Theresa May's government is intent on returning Britain's education system to a time when entry into grammar schools determined whether you lived in the comfort of a middle-class life or in the sweat of the working-class world.

Since I was born in the shadow of the Great War, society has made enormous strides in the advancement of technology and medicine. Humanity can now splice the genome, build artificial intelligent life and prolong our existence with pharmaceutical medicine. What I just don't understand is that for every step forward we make in science, we seem to take two steps back socially. We are becoming as primitive as the gas-lit world of my youth because we still refuse to eradicate greed and poverty through progressive taxation reform. Inequality is so bad today that full-time work no longer guarantees a person's escape from poverty and that spells the return to the Britain of my youth, which was a truly dog-eat-dog world.

My past is not yet your future but the eventuality of it hangs in the balance because democracy is no longer serving the needs of all its citizens. Across the globe a rising tide of strongman politics has soaked society in a hailstorm of hate and bigotry. Social media has connected more people than ever before in human history but it has divided more because these platforms have been overwhelmed by propaganda, racism, fake news or, as the new American government likes to call it, alternative facts. People today are as susceptible to the allure of a new Hitler or Lenin because, even though they have more information at their fingertips than my generation ever did to disprove the lies of these new political hatemongers, they choose to be ignorant of history.

As life runs from my body like the last dregs of a good wine from a bottle, I have tried to connect and interpret the events, the people, the love and the loneliness I have encountered on my journey.

All of humanity – me, you, your children, all who you love – are granted just a short time to savour life and gain some wisdom from existence before we are no more than photographs trapped in trunks that store trinkets and memories from long ago.

The past seems closer to me now than the future because I have only a few brief breaths left to take on this earth. All my deeds, or at least the ones that define me as a son, a brother, a soldier, an employee, a husband, friend and father, were done a long time ago. Now, I am like a star that someone sees up in the dark winter sky; all my brilliant light burned a long time ago in a far-off place.

But while I am here, I will use whatever time I have left to remember the years of my youth that were spent in inhumane poverty because our British society in the early twentieth century was divided unequally between the elite and the downtrodden.

Those memories from my early life are proof to me that today's Britain doesn't have to live under the yoke of austerity. The young today can, like my generation, become activists and join trade unions and political parties to compel our government to make society benefit all of its inhabitants, not just the lucky few born to economic privilege. Today's youth will have to mobilise their fight for social justice through social media, memes, online protests and any other new device or app used for mass communication.

Right now, Britain and the world are at the most dangerous juncture since the 1930s. We have become enamoured by the escapism populist politics provides where we can fit the blame of our woes on migrants or big institutions, which is why the European Union referendum was not an exercise in democracy but in Tory cynicism. Sadly, we the people will pay a heavy cost for the brinkmanship of David Cameron and the machinations of Farage, Gove and Johnson. Brexit will be Britain's tragedy but the election of Donald Trump as president is a calamity the whole world will be forced to bear. His actions will reverberate through the world and make Brexit and our government's continuing policy of austerity more punitive to those of our citizens who can least afford it. Democracy, society and our very core beliefs of compassion and decency have all been threatened by the forces that unleashed both Brexit and Trump.

It's why I want my grandchildren and people much younger than myself to know that we have faced these challenges before, and all is not lost. We have stood up against tyranny, against oppression both social and economic, and we have been victorious. We have resisted the darkness that comes to societies that are decayed by their contempt for democracy. We as a people will always persevere because I've seen the sun rise over Britain when the working class and middle class strived together to make a more perfect society.

I have witnessed governments in the past use fair legislation to end the greed of elites that grew across early twentieth-century society like mould on old bread. The power of justice, the endurance of hope as well as humanity's thirst for fair play and a right to have a say in how their lives are led will always triumph, no matter how long the forces of darkness reign. We must remember that Hitler didn't last, nor Stalin; imperial colonies disappeared and the Iron Curtain fell. Essentially, humanity will always stumble towards the light. I know this because I was born in the darkness of unmitigated capitalism but at the age of twenty-two helped transform Britain by voting in the 1945 general election.

I am not an academic or a historian; I am just an old man who is a living bridge to your history. Today's austerity, politics of hate and class divisions can only be defeated when the young once again own the history of their grandparents or great-grandparents' generation. My words are not a guide, a step-by-step instruction booklet on how to survive austerity; they are just lessons of hope, love and endurance from my past. This is also my testament to you about what will happen if you don't begin to defend the welfare state, which is your birth right: your ancestors sacrificed their lives in both the Great Depression and the Second World War to make Britain a green and pleasant land for everyone, not just the wealthy few.

Chapter One:
Downfall

I didn't see the defeat of the Labour Party in the May 2015 general election coming. But it came nevertheless in the early morning after polling day, when most of Britain slumbered. To many on the left, the end came with the same shock as would the unexpected death of a loved one through a car accident on the motorway. It certainly rattled me when, some time between 2.00 and 2.20 a.m. on the morning of 8 May, political pundits on every network declared Ed Miliband's ambitions to become the next Prime Minister of Britain dead. I don't think I'd emotionally invested as much in a general election since 1945. But owing to the hour, the weeks I had spent on the campaign trail, the speeches I'd given across the country in support of a progressive Labour Party that would protect our NHS from privatisation, I felt at that moment more emptiness than grief.

Downfall

All I could think was that austerity would be with us forever like a winter that refuses to yield to spring. I felt drained and a fool to have waited up to watch my dreams, and the dreams of millions of others, dashed. I thought to myself that at my age I should have been tucked up in my bed fast asleep but I wasn't. Instead, I was at a party that had been arranged for Labour Party HQ members to celebrate a victory that never came. I was in the den of a Whitehall wine bar that reminded me more of an air-raid bunker than a boozer.

It hadn't been my first election party that night – I'd gone to several to hopefully feel in the emotions of the crowd that same enthusiasm my generation felt in the summer of 1945 when Labour won that general election.

But it wasn't to be. By ten o'clock that evening the exit polls had foretold that Labour's political fortunes were done. So, when I arrived at this last election party around midnight, the mood among the guests was already lugubrious. The guests' drunkenness looked both pained and desperate. It was pure and simple disbelief mixed with fear, which bubbled over them and left them disoriented.

Neither the drink nor even the late hour allowed anyone in this bar to forget that Labour had lost the election to the Conservatives not by an inch but by a mile.

Labour's defeat was so absolute that even the possibility of a hung parliament evaporated over the course of the night; the Tories won a slim majority of twelve seats in the House of Commons. The left and centre, with the exception of the Scottish National Party, had been savaged by the electorate. The Liberal Democrats were reduced to eight seats as punishment for being either too reluctant or too willing to play dance partner to David Cameron's austerity waltz. Every Labour Party functionary who was in that wine bar with me was painfully aware that tomorrow and every other day to come for another five years belonged to the Tories and their vision for Britain. Meanwhile, the vote for UKIP on the more extreme right had risen from 3.1 per cent to 12.6 per cent since 2010.

At the moment of defeat, all around the wine bar Labour workers commiserated in small packs, texting drunkenly, fumbling for words to express a grief writ large by too many sleepless nights and a stomach full of Pinot Grigio.

On their faces, flushed with drink and disappointment, I saw the pain of the Labour Party across the many decades of my life: 1951, 1977, 1982, 2010. The style of haircut and clothes might have changed but not the look of abject sorrow on the faces of those who had put their heart and soul into fighting for ideas they thought would transform our nation for the better.

So it goes, I whispered to myself. But then my heart began to ache for the millions of people who wanted this election to put an end to austerity before it rubbed away their social safety net and their aspirations.

It was time for me to leave what had become a funeral wake at the wine bar and return to my budget hotel. Outside, the air was cool and fresh with the approach of morning. I breathed it deep into my lungs and remembered how many times through my life I had tasted the sweetness of the early morning. I knew that taste as a lad in Bradford when my family did dead-of-night runners before the landlord seized our scant possessions because of rent arrears. The air then, like on that night of Labour's loss, was pure.

A black cab picked me up and drove me across a London that dozed in the shadow of its somnolent skyscrapers. Those giant buildings of glass and steel stood as silent as clay soldiers entombed in a Chinese emperor's mausoleum. However, while the city lay recumbent, pundits on LBC spoke like commentators at an FA cup final. In caffeinated voices, people said Labour was finished and needed both new management and new players. Little did I know then how much Labour's game board would be changed by this election defeat. None of the old guard would be permitted a crack at leadership because of the sheer enormity of defeat. As my black cab floated across the deserted streets of our capital towards King's Cross and my hotel, I knew this was a turning point for the party I've loved since my youth. I just didn't realise that it would cause so much upheaval that, two years after the election, Labour's prospects would be worse than when the votes were tabulated in 2015.

I yawned and stared through the taxi window to try to gain some perspective on the night and the long election. I watched the rough sleepers toss and turn on beds made of worn cardboard and it reminded me of my youth when I saw the derelicts of Barnsley, Bradford and Halifax during the Great Depression, living rough in abandoned buildings like men cast off from civilisation.

The homeless on that election night were bathed in an uncomfortable canopy of human-made ambient light. It drifted downwards from empty office buildings and streaked the surrounding dead pavement in a dusky pale afterglow. The rough sleepers seemed to be shadowy spectres from an underworld of the dispossessed.

Driving past them, I thought, *I hope tonight you have sweet dreams because come the morrow your lives will have just got a little more precarious.* Everyone who had already been dealt a bad hand of cards in life was now on very thin ice.

Come morning, all who have been buggered in Britain by a system that rewards the wealthy and punishes the poor, the vulnerable, the disabled and the disadvantaged would know that the Tories were here to stay for another five years and that they had unfinished business with the civilised state. The result also set the clock running on David Cameron's manifesto pledge to hold a referendum on our continued membership in the European Union. However, that night no rational person could have believed that, in a little more than a year, the people of Britain would vote for the greatest momentous change in the way our nation does business and interacts with Europe because of an erroneous pledge on the side of a bus that leaving the EU would free up funds for our NHS.

In the dead of night, while the cab sped through amber traffic lights, I felt afraid – not for myself because growing up before the welfare state came into existence had done all the harm it could to do me a lifetime ago. No, I feared for all those who just had the simple desire to exist with a decent job, a roof over their head, food in their belly and smiles on their children's faces.

I couldn't see now how that could be achieved for the ordinary people of Britain. The 2015 general election guaranteed our descent back to the dog-eat-dog world of my youth, when our nation turned its back on the working class and let most of them fend for themselves in the feral era of the Great Depression. Like then, ordinary folk would suffer under the economic priorities of Cameron's Tories, who wanted the state to get smaller while the wealth of the few got bigger.

Weary, I asked the driver to turn off the radio. Knackered by the early hour, I felt like my hopes for a better Britain with a Labour government had soared past like a rescue plane that hasn't spotted survivors on a life raft in the middle of the Pacific. I felt utterly alone. I started to feel the wet dabs of self-pity immerse my reason. I couldn't work out how the opinion polls, which had predicted a minority government for either Labour or the Conservatives, could have been so incorrect. But then again, on that night, none of this country's political gurus understood how our modern-day runes had been so hopelessly wrong – even Paddy Ashdown swore he'd eat his hat if the exit polls were right.

It had been so different seventy years ago in July 1945, when Britain cast its ballot for a Labour government intent on representing Britain, not just the 1 per cent. But on that night in May 2015, the 1945 election and the optimism it inspired in my generation seemed a long time ago.

You see, I was certain of two things as I rode in that lonely cab – David Cameron was intent on changing Britain more than any twentieth-century Conservative prime minister had ever imagined, and he would use austerity as a cudgel to destroy the NHS, our education system and all of our other social services. What I didn't know was that Cameron would be swept away by the chaos he'd created by instigating the EU referendum to placate the Eurosceptics in his party.

The defeat of Labour in 2015 pulled a thread in the fabric of society, which caused Britain to unravel through Brexit. After five years of austerity and a growing north–south divide, Labour should have won the election. But it didn't and the reasons for that are many. In large part, Labour's inability to be truthful to the voter in respect of its sins in Iraq as well as its love affair with deregulating the City, along with its taking for granted that Scotland would always be a Labour stronghold, doomed the party to defeat. Labour failed to define and defend its virtues in creating not only the welfare state but a more tolerant nation. It tried to be all things to all people and in the end disappointed just about everyone. It was a tragedy for Britain that Labour lost that election because, despite all of the party's flaws, our nation would be much more universally prosperous, fair and outward-looking today with Ed Miliband as prime minister rather than Theresa May.

With many British people suffering under the Tories, Labour still only won 232 seats, its worst general election result since 1987. Labour's defeat unleashed furies that some foretold but few wanted to believe. I, for one, did not think that Labour could sink any lower than it did with those dismal election returns. Yet in a very short time it did just that because factions within the party struggled for supremacy. The party aired grievances and, like an angry plaintiff in a divorce case, spewed its discontent to all who would listen. Labour came to weep on the nation's cold and indifferent shoulder.

Peace did not come to Labour or the left wing with the election of Jeremy Corbyn as the party's new leader in September 2015. Instead, his election ushered in an acrimonious civil war that reminded me of Labour in the 1930s, when factions argued while the people starved. Corbyn is respected by many who hold the cause of social justice close to their hearts, including me, but there is an equal number of people who do not share their faith that he will deliver not only victory but a better tomorrow. Or so was the prevailing opinion of most pundits and ordinary citizens in the first months of 2017 before the snap general election in the spring of that year. In fact, in February, when Labour was 18 per cent behind the Conservatives and, for the first time in thirty-five years the opposition lost a seat to the party of government, many believed the writing was on the wall for Jeremy Corbyn as well as the Labour Party.

Even my own faith in Corbyn's leadership began to wane because I was still deeply disappointed by his ineffectual, if not indifferent, EU referendum campaign. And make no mistake: for whatever reason, Corbyn wasn't energised during the EU referendum like he had been during his first leadership race the year before or in his subsequent battle to remain leader following the referendum.

In fact, I witnessed his low-wattage campaign first-hand when I was invited by Labour to speak at a pro-Remain EU rally in Cornwall before Jeremy Corbyn addressed the crowd. Corbyn's speech was flat, disjointed and, quite frankly, disengaged. On that day, I thought he might have been tired or distracted by the media that was always biting at his trouser leg. But at every subsequent event, many others commented in either the press or personally to me that his heart didn't seem to be in the EU. When Corbyn ordered a three-line whip in February 2017 to ensure Labour supported Theresa May's Article 50 Bill triggering Brexit, I felt disheartened for both Labour's future and that of the country. I thought at the time Labour was setting itself up to be tarred by the electorate when Brexit fails to deliver the economic promises made by those who advocated for Leave on the left side of the political spectrum. However, I am aware that this tactic did much to convince many Leave voters to stick with Labour during the surprise 2017 general election.

Also, I am very aware that no one should be under the impression that Jeremy Corbyn lost the referendum for the country: that fault lies squarely with David Cameron. That's why I did not support the Parliamentary Labour Party's uprising against Corbyn in the summer of the referendum vote. In fact, feelers by disaffected MPs were sent out to me to see if I would join the coup and support Owen Smith, but I rebuffed those entreaties. I knew removing Jeremy Corbyn and replacing him with someone not fully committed to ending austerity, curbing neo-liberalism and providing a better society for all would harm the party that brought us the welfare state. As far as I was concerned, if the coup was successful, it would have destroyed Labour's chance to be considered a party for the working class for a generation to come. Moreover, I wasn't prepared to denounce Jeremy as some others did because I knew his ideas were sound and he was a decent man placed in the unenviable position of being jeered at by the right-wing press as well as people that claimed to have the Labour Party's best interests at heart.

It is unwise of us to make Jeremy Corbyn a scapegoat for a catastrophe like Brexit because it was long in the making and unleashed on us by a very cynical Tory party. The Labour heartlands weren't lost by Corbyn; they were lost by thirty years of economic and social policies that have decimated hope in Britain's once mighty industrial regions. But Labour must bear some responsibility in turning working-class hearts cold to its belief in Europe and in multiculturalism. We just didn't have any contingency plan to alleviate the hardship that globalisation placed upon working-class families who didn't have the skills or education to survive an end to industrial factory work. The simple and tragic fact that MP Jo Cox's assassination by a right-wing fanatic radicalised by fascism and fake news did not deter her constituency from overwhelmingly voting for Brexit, tells you the referendum was lost long before the ballot papers were even printed.

By the end of the campaign, which had seen me criss-cross England, Wales and Northern Ireland to speak to gatherings about why the EU was Britain's best option, I knew in the pit of my stomach that the referendum was lost. That's why, on the night of 23 June 2016, I was alone. I preferred to have only the company of the BBC reporting back to me, in the dark hours of morning, that Britain's relationship with the European Union had unravelled.

That vote will change not only our nation's history but our own personal histories as well. We are irrevocably altered. The fight against austerity and neo-liberalism has become a lot harder since we decided to leave the EU. Let's be clear, the institution was far from perfect: it needed reform, democratisation and a return to social democratic principles. But walking away from the EU during a normal time would have been dangerous; in the era of Donald Trump, it may prove to be a disaster too large for a nation to withstand.

We are in most dangerous waters because of Brexit and nothing that we once took for granted, such as peace in

Europe, a public NHS and Scotland as a nation within the United Kingdom, can be assured. Moreover, we mustn't delude ourselves into thinking that just because the Tories have been reduced to a minority in parliament that somehow Brexit will be managed for the benefit of workers. Essentially, any which way you slice Brexit, it is a rotten apple. It's why I am concerned that if in the next two years the Tory party's government should fall, Labour will be handed the Brexit negotiations, which may prove to be a poisoned chalice. Everything political, economic and social is up for grabs and this terrifies me. It's why, even though I am jubilant that Labour under Jeremy Corbyn was able to battle Theresa May in the recent snap election and turn her once workable majority into a hung parliament, I still worry about Brexit. You see, even a soft Brexit is a dangerous course to take and it will provide many challenges to the people of this country that were perhaps best left untested. Now, on the crest of summer 2017, Britain's economy is hurting, real wage growth doesn't exist for the average worker and inflation now tops 2.9 per cent because of Brexit.

I fear that Britain is walking into many seasons of discontent and Labour cannot hide if it wants to serve the many and not the few. These unsettling times, the rise in hatred and the spectre of poverty have driven my thoughts right back to the 1920s and my childhood.

Chapter Two:
A Destiny of Poverty

A winter's rain fell outside the tenement house where I was born into the Smith family on 25 February 1923 in Barnsley. That night, everywhere near and far from our doorstep, hunger and famine prowled like feral animals the streets of working-class Britain. Prosperity had not come to our country after defeating the Kaiser's army in 1918 – only recession – and, after five years of peace, the working people of Britain were on the point of defeat from wages that wouldn't allow them to make ends meet. The Great War was so fresh in everyone's memory that it cast a heavy shadow across the country both economically and spiritually. Victorious we may have been, but the cost in human life and to our economy seemed insuperable. In the same manner that the calamity of our war in Iraq in 2003 or our eternal war on terrorism have scarred a generation and curtailed economic advancement for so many citizens, the Great War did that to my parents' generation and to their children. It's depressing to think what Britain could have done to make a better society with the £34 billion spent on our participation in wars in Afghanistan and Iraq, whose outcomes many would argue have made the world less secure.

The 1920s was a time of grim misery for the common folk and my family lived in the thick of it. My kin worked, procreated, slept and died in a slum that collected around the edge of a Barnsley coal pit like gangrene forms near an infected open wound. At the coal mine, my dad toiled in inhumane conditions for his crust of bread, knowing that was the best he would ever get out of life.

Our neighbourhood was a place where one lived to work until you were too old or injured to earn your keep and then you died. It lacked both beauty and empathy. Had social and economic change not come after the Second World War, my fate would have been very much like all my ancestors since the dawn of the Industrial Revolution and no better than slavery. I would have lived and eventually died in a miserable hovel similar to the one where I was born. In between my birth and my death, I would have spent my allotted time on earth like a beast of burden toiling beneath the earth, hacking at the coal face with a pick, in miserable conditions for pitiable wages, just like my dad and granddad did. I would have dug coal until my body was too injured from poverty and excruciating manual labour, whereupon my employment would have been terminated. If I was lucky, my kinfolk would have cared for me in my premature old age while my sons took my place at the coal face hundreds of feet beneath the earth's surface.

My mum, whose character was made from Yorkshire stone that could cut your knee when you just glanced at it, once said to me that the miserable weather that fell hard against our slate roof on the night of my birth 'was a warning to thee of the shite to come in your life and mine'.

As I grew, my mum often told me the tale of my birth in an effort to prove her motherly worth, even if she couldn't properly feed or clothe me through most of my childhood. 'Aye,' she said, 'you hollered like a stuck pig when you came from my belly – nothing soothed you. But I don't blame you for bawling because it was a cold night and you were hungry. Besides, by the look you wore on your face, you knew that this bloody world was going to give you nowt.'

My mother wasn't exaggerating when she said, 'It was like you were born with the mark of Cain on your forehead because you came into a family of poor folk who didn't even have two farthings to scratch together.'

I was born on a mattress made of flock in a dingy room lit by candles. A midwife, whose face was flushed red from her penchant for her gin, attended to my mother, Lillian. My mum swore and cursed through my delivery because, as my gran told me later on, 'You were a nipper who just didn't want to face the world.'

My dad, Albert, sat stoically on a stool near a lukewarm coal fire that sputtered in our scullery oven on the ground

26

floor. He patiently waited for my cries of life as he had done for my two elder sisters Marion and Alberta, who played games on a cold, rough cement floor that had small mats, made from knotted rags, scattered about it.

As the midwife cut the umbilical cord from my mother with a sharp razor and swaddled me in old cloth that had been boiled clean on the stove, the world outside was in foment. Britain was in a time of recession and her industrial regions lay dormant while unemployment shook the economic stability of society. Everywhere in Europe, there was either revolution or reaction to it. Russia was in the hands of the Bolsheviks and Germany was in riot. At home, British workers questioned the value of their sacrifice to King and Country when their reward was either unemployment or substandard wages from unscrupulous employers.

To this day, I do not know if my birth was planned or an accident. But I do know that in the era of my arrival contraception was a rare luxury except for the rich. Moreover, women, despite the fact that some had been afforded the right to vote in 1919, were still considered to be chattel to a man's desires and demands. So, no matter how strong-willed and stubborn my mother was, society dictated that she would always be under the thumb of men. All my mum could do in retaliation to those who kept her in servitude, whether it was her father, her brothers, former suitors, my dad or her future lovers, was establish her sovereignty through either sarcasm or sex appeal.

It's hard to know if my mum and dad loved one another when they married in June 1914 just before the start of the First World War. They had married because my mother had become pregnant and society did not look kindly on an unwed mother. It was a marriage that began in tragedy because my mother lost her first child in a miscarriage. Sadly, their lives did not really improve as the seventeen years they were together caused them more anguish than joy owing to their poverty. By the time of my arrival, their affection for each other had begun to sour like milk because it had been tested too often by the brutality of living skint on a miner's wage.

But keeping love strong today is just as tough for some young couples struggling on intern wages in London or zero-hour contracts up north. According to the Resolution Foundation, real hourly wages for those in their twenties are down 12 per cent since 2008. At the same time, the cost of living has gone up: rail fares have increased by 21 per cent, rent by 11 per cent, electricity by 28 per cent, gas by 38 per cent and food by 13 per cent. Austerity has played havoc with the normal running of our society and the young are paying a heavy price for it as the gig economy strips them of financial security.

I am amazed that I made it out of my mother's womb alive. So much in the 1920s could go wrong for both mother and child in Britain before the NHS, especially if you didn't have the money to pay for a doctor in case of complications during the pregnancy.

A Destiny of Poverty

It is hard to imagine now but when my mother was expecting me or any of her other children, she saw no doctor because my father's wages, despite the fact that he worked six days a week, ten hours a day, could not stretch to that luxury. When my mother carried me in her womb, there was no pre-natal care for expectant mothers or visits from a district nurse. Those services just didn't exist for working-class mothers.

Today, because of both the coalition government and now Theresa May's government, antenatal and postnatal care have been drastically curtailed due to an ideologically driven austerity policy. In fact, a report by the Royal College of Midwives in October 2015 concluded that over two-fifths of maternity units in England had to close down temporarily during the previous twelve months because they couldn't cope with the demand; it is estimated that the country requires an additional 2,600 midwifes adequately to service pregnant mothers. Moreover, austerity is forcing NHS trusts to centralise services, which may mean the permanent closure of many maternity wards. Proposals may lead to pregnant mothers in Cumbria having to travel forty miles from Whitehaven to Carlisle; depending on the time of day and weather conditions, it can take upwards of two hours to travel between the two locations – thereby the lives and welfare of mothers and babies will be at greater risk. Unless austerity is curtailed, there will come a time in the near future when childbirth for the working poor in this country may be as difficult as it was for my mother.

My mum often told me that, as a child, 'you were like the runt in a herd of pigs, mewling for milk because you were sore, hungry and sickly. Weren't the midwife that kept you alive, it was the fire I breathed into thee to keep you warm because nothing kept you from death but thy mother's love and determination that you were not to be taken to the knackers' yard until you are an old man and good for nowt.'

It's true that I was an underweight bairn but that was because, since the end of the First World War, miners' wages had been depressed and that meant my parents had little money to ensure that my mum had sufficient nutrients to feed herself and me growing inside her.

Looking back, it was a miracle that I made it past my first birthday. Once born, the world was a deadly place in the 1920s for a child raised in poverty because society didn't see it as its responsibility to care for the health and well-being of the nation's children. Years afterwards, when my first son was born in 1955, my mother ruefully commented after I mentioned how long my wife was in labour that, had she been able to deliver her children in a hospital rather than in the squat we called home, she'd have taken a right long time, too.

On the day of my birth in 1923, there were no congratulations to Lillian from her siblings, no fanfare at my arrival from friends or neighbours, no glad-handing down at the pub for Albert's first son. There was no announcement in the local newspaper. It wasn't a moment for celebration;

it was a time for dread because my existence meant that another mouth was demanding to be fed in a family that couldn't make ends meet.

Years after, my mum said to me, 'I didn't know who cried more when you were born, me or you, because I knew your life was damned from the start as you were the son of a Barnsley miner.' Today, it is no better for the people of Barnsley because no matter how hard they work, in that city their wages are about 15 per cent lower than the national average. I am not surprised that places like Barnsley and many other regions that are as economically depressed as South Yorkshire voted for Brexit, as they were forgotten by Labour when they were in power and ignored by the Tories who now govern. But the belief that Brexit for Barnsley or Stoke or anywhere else will bring back good-paying jobs is a chimera. It's not the EU or migrants that depress wages and mothball industries but a neo-liberal ideology that allows for globalisation without proper checks or balances on corporations. This, with massive subsidies to British corporations and cutbacks to the social safety network, has allowed our nation's heartlands to rust and decay like an abandoned car at a disused scrapyard.

While I slept on that first night of my life, Britain tossed and turned with distress. Much of the country was either in recession or trying to recover from the destruction that the Great War had wrought upon our people. Death lingered like a sickly perfume in the houses of the working class, middle class and well-to-do because so much blood had been spilled that it soaked into the everyday lives of people. It touched my family because my mum had lost her eldest brother and my dad many cousins.

As I grew, teethed and learned to crawl on the rough stone floors of our scullery, our economic situation grew direr because, as the price of coal fell, so did my father Albert's pay packet. My dad struggled to keep a roof over our heads. The simple fact was that his pay was a pittance even before the price of coal crashed through the floor in the 1920s; but afterwards he made less than a pound a week. During that era, a family needed at least a pound a week to keep their heads above water, so trying to live off 80p was like trying to breathe while six inches underwater.

While I was still feeding from my mother's breasts our life was as precarious as migratory beasts during a time of drought. I think that while I drank her milk, I also digested all her angst, all her worries about the survival of herself, her husband and her brood of children because I am still haunted by those early years of privation and how it ultimately damaged my mother's psychology along with the rest of our family. The sort of stress my mother encountered trying to keep her children from harm during those tough economic times has returned to afflict many vulnerable families trying to raise their children in marginalised neighbourhoods in David Cameron and Theresa May's Britain. A report in 2016 by a UN committee condemned the Tory government for putting more citizens into economically vulnerable situations since 2010 because of their policy of austerity. It found that too many families on low incomes were reliant on food banks because they had become impoverished by unaffordable rental accommodation. The report concluded that the lack of affordable housing, combined with a minimum wage that was not a real living wage, put excessive financial pressure on the marginalised.

What happened to our country nine decades ago was disastrous for the likes of my family and what is happening now will be for you in this new era of entitlement for the few and pain for the many. The results of austerity are all around us today: statistics tell us that rough sleeping has increased by 16 per cent since 2015. But the numbers don't tell of the real suffering, which you find on your high street when you look to the pavement to find the young and the middle-aged who have nowhere to call home wrapped in thin sleeping bags, offering us a God bless for a few bits of coin.

In the decade of my birth, the costs of even renting a hovel were extravagant. Everyone who wasn't upper middle class or wealthier was affected because the lean times stretched from our squalid street to every cesspool, dilapidated tenement, run-down cottage and festering flat in the country. My family, friends and strangers all had a similar story of endurance: of doing without, of surviving because the alternative was to die in the street. It is not difficult to understand the plight my generation faced in the 1920s. The family picture albums that you keep tucked away in a cupboard or a drawer will reveal to you the pain of my generation. In them you should be able to find any number of haunting sepia-toned images of one of your dead ancestors looking out to eternity with disbelief at how hard life can be if you are working class.

Later on, when the Great Depression struck, I would sometimes cry myself to sleep because the physical pain from lack of food in my belly was too intense for my young mind to comprehend. 'Unless we become beggars, tears won't feed you, lad,' my mum would rail at me with an anger that she wanted to direct at the world outside.

Having been indentured into work at the age of twelve, my mother had learned the hard way that, for the less fortunate, 'It's only a cat's cunning that lets you escape danger.' But my mum's craft at keeping our family's heads above water was only so good. It certainly was sorely tested by the general strike of 1926 when my father was on the picket lines for over eight months. Sometimes, no matter her determination to keep us going, there was nothing more she could do except water down our oatmeal until it resembled soup rather than porridge.

Lack of food, poor sanitation and bad health were the birth right of Britain's working poor in the early twentieth century. It is why my family would always know famine and never feasting until the election of the Labour government in 1945.

When my mother told me about my struggles to remain alive as a toddler, she said, 'You were poorly so many times, I began to believe you weren't sure if life was quite right for thee. It was like you were a cat testing the water by the river's edge and you weren't certain if it was too hot or too cold for your liking.'

Without a doubt, it was Lillian's defiance against my mortality that kept me alive because bouts of diarrhoea as a baby had left me weak and susceptible to all manner of illness and, as there was no NHS, my survival depended upon her determination that none of her children would die before her. As she said, 'No one else gave a toss for thee.' After the Second World War, when I returned home on leave from being stationed in Hamburg as part of the occupational forces, I remember that my mum stared at me in uniform and said, 'Look at what grew out of the muck of my life: a right handsome lad.'

As a teen, when the storms of the Great Depression began to pass and I started to question the harsh and unsavoury methods my mum used to survive that economic calamity, she'd silence me with invective, spite and her only legitimate defence: 'Hate me all you will, but I saved your life. Forget not, lad, that when you were a bairn and your intestines kept dribbling out of your backside like a stuck pig, I didn't call the knackers or fetch a spade and bury you out back in the midden. I just pushed 'em back in the hole and said you ain't going to die until you're long in the tooth and don't know where the chairs are in thy room.'

Sadly, no matter what fire my mum tried to breathe into my elder sister Marion's lungs, it did no good because she developed spinal tuberculosis from the unsanitary slums that we called home. My earliest memories, flickering in my mind like shadows illuminated by sputtering gaslight, are always of sickness and the approaching death of Marion.

After all these years, I can still see her wasting away in our cramped one-up one-down terraced house. The disease had made her an invalid so she was imprisoned on a wicker bed that had wheels, which allowed my mother to push her outside and enjoy the sun caressing her face. Otherwise, Marion was marooned in our parlour, which was a squat, grimy room that was starved of natural light because the window was just a crevice.

Disease, sickness, lack of money and poor living conditions ensured ours wasn't a happy household. My parents spent many a night arguing over money, over regrets, over the slow death of their eldest daughter.

But our unhappiness as a family wasn't unique because extreme malnutrition or diseases like diphtheria, rickets and tuberculosis came with the same ferocity and cruelty as the plague did to peasant neighbourhoods in the seventeenth century. Each tiny tenement house was its own universe of familial despair and disappointment all predicated on one simple reality: the ordinary people of Britain were too poor to afford happiness. It was a theft of joy by the elites who didn't want to pay their fair share to society and this attitude has returned to Britain over these last few years. Some breadwinners must now work two or three jobs to keep the wolf from the door while our more affluent citizens are receiving record tax breaks to make their lives more comfortable.

A Destiny of Poverty

What disturbed my parents the most as they tried to alleviate my sister's agony was that they knew more affluent victims of this disease could survive the affliction if properly treated through medical therapies and well-equipped sanatoriums. Ultimately, what determined whether TB moved quickly from chronic to terminal was whether you could afford a lifestyle that kept death at bay.

Unfortunately, TB, like typhus or diphtheria, was more at home in the filth and muck of the dank warrens where the poor of my boyhood dwelled. As my sister Marion had lived exclusively in ramshackle housing that was replete with vermin, lice and filth, she simply didn't have the strength to combat her tuberculosis like a child from a middle-class family.

Nothing better illustrates that, before the NHS, longevity and good healthcare was determined by where one stood in Britain's class system than to compare Marion's life to that of the politician Tony Benn's younger brother. The boy's illness was almost identical to my sister's but for one important factor: the Benns were wealthy, which meant Tony's sibling could be treated with the best possible care money could buy. While Marion died, Tony's brother survived.

Here lies the rub for modern British society if it does not possess an adequately funded and comprehensive social safety net: life and death become dependent upon one's bank balance, instead of what should be a universal principle that all humans irrespective of class, income, education or purpose deserve decent medical care. No social justice can exist in a culture that accepts the notion that a child from a wealthy family deserves to survive whereas a child from the slums does not. Essentially that is a prejudice that is as vile as racial bigotry or misogyny.

I was very young when Marion died but I still recall playing near her sickbed as if it happened an hour ago. As a small boy, I thought of her more as an angel who watched over me rather than an elder sister. I guess this was because she was never able to speak to me because the disease had robbed her of a voice. Marion may have been silent but she was not stoical to the overwhelming pain she endured.

In fact, Marion's illness was so severe and her discomfort so pronounced, so violent and so bitter that my dad restrained her to the bed with ropes. In the end, when death approached, my mum and dad hoped to ease Marion's suffering by taking her to a workhouse infirmary that loomed over our neighbourhood like the gates of hell. She went there because my parents believed she would be given at least some medicine to ease her passage from this life to what they believed was a better place.

It was there she died on a miserable day in October 1926. As my parents had no savings because every penny my dad received was spent on food and the rent for our subhuman accommodation, my sister was buried without ceremony in a paupers' pit. Marion was forgotten quicker by society than if she had been a dog hit by a car in today's Britain.

We still have an NHS but only just because, since 2010, it has been placed in chronic crisis by the government and a secretary of state for health who seems intent on starving our hospitals and our doctors of the funds they need to provide more than adequate service. The Care Quality Commission's 'State of Care in NHS Acute Hospitals' report, published in early 2017, shows that, after inspections of 136 acute non-specialist hospital trusts in England and all 18 specialist trusts, the situation is grim. The report found that 9 per cent of acute trusts were rated as inadequate, while 59 per cent were told they required improvement; in terms of safety standards, 81 per cent of acute trusts were inadequate or required improvement. The simple fact is that the NHS has some of the finest doctors, nurses and support staff in the world but once the government begins to curtail adequate spending on healthcare, the system will begin to break down and that will eventually lead to dire consequences.

Chapter Three:

At the Doorstep of Homelessness

On my many recent trips across Britain, I've seen on a few occasions families being put into the street by a bailiff, which is not surprising because in 2015 there were 15,000 such occurrences. But I have also seen, while I pass through traumatised neighbourhoods, those families not yet evicted who put all their possessions in a car and drive away in a desperate bid to find better luck in another rundown part of their town.

When it comes to housing we have moved beyond crisis in twenty-first-century Britain and snuggled up to catastrophe. Low wages along with curtailed government benefits have made over 82,000 tenants two months in arrears on their rent. It's worse for social credit tenants: three in four of them are in serious arrears for their lodgings.

What is that saying again? All that is old is new again?

At the Doorstep of Homelessness

The problem people face today was faced by their ancestors before the welfare state. I am living proof of this because I remember our flits. In January 1927, my family moved lodgings at the black hour of midnight, and not for the last time. We upped sticks in the freezing darkness because my dad just wasn't able to pay our landlord his due.

That first time when we disappeared under dark clouds, my dad tapped my shoulder to wake me as I slept with my sister on a filthy mattress that stank of other people's piss and sweat. My eyes were still eager for sleep but my father motioned with a finger placed to his lips to be silent and then whispered in my ear that I must be quick. My sister and I jumped from our bed, still dressed in shabby clothes provided to us by a local charity. We quietly shuffled downstairs in confused fright and into the cold night air.

Outside, my mother first hugged both of us and then led us across pavements dusted with snow with the protectiveness of a feral mother cat who marshals her brood through another feline's territory. My dad, in shame over our flight from rent debt, trailed behind because my mother's invective against him acted like a headwind slowing him down.

We didn't take much with us on that cold winter's night in 1927. All we took was what we could put into sacks and carry on our backs, like modern-day migrants. On our way to our new domicile, I remember holding in my hand a cheap metal toy train that had been given to me for Christmas by my parents only a few weeks previous. At the time, I didn't know that it would be the last gift I would ever receive from my parents in childhood. If I'd been aware, I probably would have held it even tighter to my heart.

The piano that my father loved to play in order to soothe Marion while she angrily fought death was left abandoned in our former parlour. It was too large and cumbersome to drag through the quiet night-time streets of our slum. Anyway, I suppose it would have also been too painful for my dad to see the piano in our new surroundings because it would have been a constant reminder that he was parted from his daughter forever.

In an act of sentimentality or defiance against our fate, my dad brought with him an oil portrait of his father that was held in an ornate gilded frame, which indicated that at one time our family had the luxury of adorning the walls of our home with painted mementoes of much-loved relatives. Along with the portrait, my father carried in a coal sack an eight-volume edition of the *Harmsworth History of the World*. My dad might have dug coal for his living but he yearned for knowledge like others craved material wealth.

I also think he took those objects with us so that my sister Alberta and I would know that, even though he'd been undone by an unequal economy, he once had greater ambitions and prospects for himself than fighting like an animal for scraps of food to keep his family fed. It was his legacy to teach us that, even when things are at their worst, we must hold on to civilisation. For him civilisation was a picture of his father and a history about the marvels of ancient empires. As for today, what must we hold on to in order to believe in our civilisation?

My mother, however, was more grounded in the muck of Yorkshire and, until my dad disappeared from our lives some years later, she mocked his attachment to those books and that painting of his father. 'It would be best if you pitched those books into the fire to keep us warm,' she told him on a particularly cold evening. 'And, while you're at it, throw your miserable old sod of a dad on to the grate with them.'

Years after, in the dying days of the Second World War, I remember watching refugees wearing ragged clothing and broken shoes amble on the gravel shoulder of a dual carriageway as my RAF unit moved into northern Germany. As I saw them moving in dejected columns in a desperate bid to find safety, they reminded me in some way of my family, when we were also in search of a safe place to rest.

Being homeless in many ways is like being orphaned because your moorings to love and security are cut and you are cast adrift into a torrent of uncertainty. As a child and teenager, I never felt secure in my housing or whether I'd be able to get a decent meal at the end of the day. Those anxieties didn't end for me until I joined the RAF in 1941. The Air Force guaranteed, at least, that if I did right by them they would return my loyalty with food, clothing and a bunk to rest my weary head. No one before my military service could ever match that pledge because society was geared to only benefit those with middle-class wealth or above.

The new tenement we fled to in Barnsley in 1927 was smaller than the hovel we had left just one hurried step ahead of the bailiff. We had to share it with an elderly, childless couple. For the first few days the fireplace grates were cold because our housemates were waiting for my parents to buy the fuel. Inside our home, the damp stuck to the walls and left a cold unpleasant odour that lingered like the stench that emanates from a dishevelled tramp you might encounter in a seedy public house, propped up against a far wall and nursing a pint of bitter.

In truth, the house we moved into was no better than a stall for an animal in a poor farmer's paddock. That we were forced to live this way in the past was unjust, but if you don't think it is happening in today's Britain, think again.

Sky News reported in 2016 that one-third of private rented homes aren't up to proper standards of health and safety. Moreover, three-quarters of a million homes are infested with rodents, are damp and have other problems that make them dangerous to dwell in. Yet the owners of these fleapits can earn a fortune in rent because twenty-first-century Britain is becoming as socially dystopian as it was in my boyhood. And the only reason why is because governments have encouraged both greed and the notion that housing is the best investment for those with disposable income, fuelling house-price and rent increases by speculation as well as a decline in affordable accommodation. Moreover, the Tory government in London and Tory councils all across the country have slashed regulations, making it easier to exploit those seeking affordable and safe housing.

As there were only two bedrooms in our new home, my family kipped together while our housemates slept in the other room. The four of us huddled on one small mattress under dirty blankets for warmth like we were rabbits packed tight in a hutch being sold at the Barnsley market.

Shortly after our arrival, the man who shared the house with us died. He'd been found dead from a heart attack in the outdoor bog. To scare me, my sister said that he'd been murdered by thugs in the bog. After that, I was petrified every time I used the toilet, thinking that I'd meet a similar fate to the old man. Not long after the man died, his widow moved out. She left one morning carrying a cardboard suitcase and much later my mother told me she'd made a vague promise, 'like a bloody sailor', to return and sort out her portion of the rent. Before she could make good on her word, my parents decided it was better for us to move on to an even less expensive and more inhospitable area. So we upped sticks again in the dead of night. We never seemed to move far from where we started, and this time we ended up near the local tip. On most days, you could smell it festering from our stoop.

My sister, being older than me, would drag me to the tip in hope of finding lost treasure. There, we scampered through its ocean of rubbish looking for something to sell or barter like children now do in Third World countries. For my sister and me, it was pop bottles we looked for that could be traded for a penny. Mostly, however, we just found discarded buttons from shirts that had rotted into rags from the sweat of hard labour. It was on these ziggurats of waste that my sister told me that I best learn how to be strong or else 'I'd be for the bone yard' like our sister Marion.

Our new neighbourhood looked like an even more dystopian, foreign land because the inhabitants were dressed in rags and women, stooped with rickets, trolled through the uneven cobbled streets and bantered in a defiant Barnsley accent that sounded more like dogs barking in irritation than human speech. To tease or frighten me, Alberta told me that the women who were bent over like trees deformed by a rough environment were witches.

In the winter of early 1928 my family was undone by its greatest calamity when my dad was seriously injured in a mining accident. He was brought home to us on a barrow pulled by two mates.

At first, my mother was relieved to see that he hadn't been killed in a cave-in like the man who lived at the top of our street had been not long before my father's mishap. For those who worked underground, where they could not see the soot-stained sky that hung low over Barnsley like a soiled sheet, death or injury at work was then a normal occurrence.

Over time, my mum's relief at my dad's survival became clouded by her rage at being saddled with a man who couldn't provide during an era when married women were not encouraged to work by the state, their families or potential employers.

'If I had been born a man,' she loved to boast when we lived rough-and-ready in a Bradford doss a few years later, 'I'd have sorted our money woes.' However, at the time six million blokes were looking for work so, had my mother been a man, she would have been as defeated as my dad was looking for a job to feed his hungry brood.

In the end, my dad probably also wished that he had died from his accident rather than linger infirm and no longer capable of hard physical labour. At first, after his accident, the pit managers put him to work doing manual labour on the surface of the mine because it was considered less strenuous.

So, for much less pay he hauled coal and shifted lumber and scrap metal, and tried as best as he could not to further injure himself. But my father's reduced salary made it even more difficult to feed us, house us and keep our hovel warm.

Even before the crash of 1929 that ushered in the Great Depression, many working families in Britain were finding it difficult to maintain their standard of living because the recession in northern England, like today's economic woes, had frozen wages while the cost of living was still dear. My parents and the rest of the lower classes were being immersed in petty debt, lack of affordable housing and work shortages that were producing malnutrition, premature death and anxiety in epidemic quantity.

Sadly, not much has changed for many families since 1928 because 3.9 million British families are just one pay cheque away from insolvency, which means that should the breadwinners of households lose their income like my dad did, their prospects in Tory Britain may become as bleak as ours were almost a century ago. In the twenty-first century, for those with precarious finances every day can be just as emotionally unsettling. Many people just don't know any more if they can keep their heads above water and that's just not right. But it is more than not right: it's a recipe for social disaster. Revolutions and civic unrest always develop after prolonged inequalities. Some, like the 1945 creation of our welfare state, are peaceful; others, like the Arab Spring in 2010, are chaotic and brutal. Whether it be in France in 1789 or Iran in 1978, inequality can lead to a reset in society that sometimes can be beneficial and other times creates authoritarianism. It's why everyone should be concerned by the 2016 presidential election in the United States because, although it was a democratic vote that made Donald Trump president and gave power to his radical views on race, trade and diplomacy, it was also a revolution that upset the normal tide of government. The same has occurred in Britain with Brexit and the question on everyone's mind is what will happen to our country once it is enacted? Will we see chaos, or progress?

Right now, the tipping point for our society might be the housing crisis. The threat of homelessness since the 2008 banking crisis has grown while the wages of the average worker have fallen. The Trades Union Congress, after analysing income data for the past nine years, has concluded that real income for average workers has declined by 1 per cent each year since 2008: that is a 9 per cent drop in earnings, whereas rent has increased over the same period by over 2 per cent, according to the Office for National Statistics. Anyone who is just an ordinary person in Britain is at risk of losing what little they've earned because, as the welfare state shrinks, housing becomes more expensive, dental care becomes unaffordable, higher education for your children becomes out of reach. In fact, if you lose your job, or you or your loved ones get sick, you are at the mercy of a system that no longer empathises with your struggles because our Tory government is more concerned with preserving the entitlement of corporations to pay as little tax as possible to the state.

In seven years of government, the Tories have slashed corporate tax from 28 per cent to 17 per cent. In that same period of government, according to the Rowntree Foundation, the number of British people living in poverty has risen to 13.5 million. Moreover, the foundation has concluded that there are over a million people in our country who are destitute and unable adequately to feed themselves or afford decent shelter. But the one person who seems more than able to find his seat at the table is the author of austerity, George Osborne. Since being removed from the Treasury by Theresa May, Osborne has secured himself a position at BlackRock, an American asset management firm, where he will act as an advisor and be paid handsomely for it.

It doesn't take a clairvoyant to know that Britain isn't walking into an equalitarian future under this Tory government.

It is being frog-marched into an economic dystopia that has an eerie resemblance to the inequality I witnessed as a boy in the 1920s and 1930s when poverty was the norm and not the exception for working-class Britain. It's why, despite all that is modern and beyond my aged grasp, I find the twenty-first century too familiar for my liking.

By the summer of 1928, my father was struggling to keep up with the physical demands of his job. He battled on like an old workhorse and every day feared dismissal. My sister and I witnessed through the humidity of summer our parents' affection for each other cool as my dad's diminished pay packet put extreme stress upon their marriage. Many times, my mum lamented to anyone who would listen that her greatest mistake in life was marrying my dad. By the time autumn had set in, my mother's love for my father was embedded in permafrost because we couldn't even afford the minimum amount of coal to keep the damp out of our bones.

In the evenings, my mother kept warm by lashing recriminations out at my dad, who sat helpless before an empty grate in the parlour. Upstairs, my sister and I hid from our parents' discord. We wrapped ourselves up underneath soiled bed covers and told each other stories about lost treasures that were buried in the rubbish tip up the road until sleep hushed our feverish imaginations. When morning came, we slipped from the world of our dreams into the cold, yellow light of day.

At one breakfast, my mother wept and asked for our forgiveness as she served us up a half portion of porridge and said there would be nothing more until tea. But our days of hunger had just begun because my dad had a hernia, which grew worse from the surface work. The union he belonged to provided him with a truss, which was the best they could do, but it was no good against the physical demands of his job and he ruptured himself again. This time there was no hope for my dad. He wasn't able to retain his job and, without ceremony, without pension and without any real hope of finding other employment, he was dismissed.

It was my dad's great tragedy that the 1926 general strike had been lost because otherwise the Miners' Federation of Great Britain (the precursor to the National Union of Mineworkers) or a local union would have been able to protect him from dismissal in 1928. It's why in this day and age, everyone must be concerned by the Trade Union Act that our Tory government passed in 2016. It now means that the rights of workers to collective action as well as to call a strike have been greatly curtailed. People should always bear this in mind when Theresa May and members of her cabinet assert that they will protect the rights of workers when Brexit comes. When our divorce from the European Union is final, be prepared to wake up into a new working world where wages and job protection are as meagre for you as they were for my dad in 1928.

The instant my father was let go from his employment, we were destitute because we had no financial reserves and my father's pay packet had never truly met even our most basic needs anyway. From the age of five until eleven, regular meals were a luxury my parents couldn't afford to give me because jobs were scarce as water in the desert and wages low. My life, although it has been long and fruitful, has ultimately been defined by a childhood that was too hard by far.

It's marked me because working-class people were treated with less concern than domestic farm animals. We were easily replaced when we became injured like my dad was in the mines. With the rise of robots in the modern workplace, the way I and my family were treated is a distinct possibility for low-wage, poorly educated workers today. In my day, the way many in the middle classes and certainly an overwhelming majority in the elite classes saw the working people of Britain was little better than the way imperial Russia viewed its serfs. We were there to build their railways and their ships, dig their coal and spin their wool into profit, and when we were no longer needed we were forgotten and left to die in the slums. The Britain of my youth was a world that wasn't uncomfortable with seeing children faint from lack of nutrients, develop rickets or perish from diseases that prey upon the malnourished. It was a society whose leaders didn't care how the other half lived and they showed great resentment when the poor and the unemployed demanded greater attention to their needs. Is it any different today, when the poor are castigated on the much-watched television programme *Benefits Street*? Those who rule us seem to do best at dehumanising us and causing divisions so that we don't have either the numbers or the strength to demand real change from our parliamentarians.

The elites that wrote the laws certainly knew how to dehumanise us in my boyhood. All the British state provided back then was an unemployment dole that was only for a short duration. It paid out a stipend that was less than the minimum needed to keep a family in food and lodgings. Once the dole was exhausted, your last resort was a local council's poor relief and that was twelve shillings a month, which was just one-third the amount needed to sustain a family of four for thirty days. So, if you were on poor relief, you were guaranteed that if you didn't die from malnutrition, you would perish from the despair of being forced to live in dilapidated housing that was squat, overcrowded, under-heated, unsanitary and rank with vermin.

That's why, on the day my dad lost his position at the mine, my mother began to lose her emotional moorings and, in bouts of despair, would say in a voice that was empty and defeated, 'If the sun don't begin to shine down on us, it's the workhouse for you two, 'cause thy father doesn't have the brass to keep you fed.'

Chapter Four:
Barnsley – Suffocated by Austerity

In my old age, I walk with trepidation on Barnsley's pavement stones, not because my balance is off but out of fear that I am like Lot's wife looking backwards at things best forgot.

All my kin are dead in this town. Now, they are just mournful shadows whose images are preserved on photographic paper pressed behind a multitude of pound-shop glass frames that are scattered around my home.

Yet, I persist in coming to visit Barnsley, like a salmon that must spawn in its birthplace. I don't know what I hope to find here. My childhood? My innocence? Or perhaps, I am looking to locate the places where the memories, which now cut so deep into my soul that I can't excise them from my consciousness, were made. But in truth, I think I return because I want to find the reasons why Britain is starting to resemble the world of my youth, making us profoundly troubled and divided today.

All the houses I lived in as a boy in this town have long since been taken down by the wrecker's ball, when slum clearance was the watchword of national and local government. The only thing that remains from those long-ago days is my grandparents' sturdy two-up one-down, which they first rented in 1901. It's where they raised their six children to become miners or the wives of miners. It's located in a neighbourhood that has been marginalised for 200 years and will never see gentrification but still wears its working-class roots with a sturdy, proud defiance.

The last time I came to Barnsley, I returned to that house where a lifetime ago my grandparents lived and died. I peered into its front window because its present-day owners were at work. I looked into a living room that bulged with plush easy chairs and a widescreen television set that dwarfed the wall, and remembered how spartan this room was in my grandparents' day. In my head, I heard the voice of my grandmother admonish me for wanting to dig up old ghosts by coming here. 'It's best to let sleeping dogs lie, because they can't hurt thee then,' she once told me vehemently when I asked her about the rumours that the child my mum was carrying in the summer of 1930 was not my dad's but another man's. Then again, my gran always wanted everything out of sight and out of mind but that was to hide her own dark secrets. Despite her Victorian petticoats and Sunday-church attitudes, my grandmother had spent a lifetime concealing from nosey neighbours that her first-born son wasn't my granddad's but the child of another man with whom she'd had a fling while my grandfather was a soldier in India.

I still find myself, despite my grandmother's warning, always kicking at the past trying to rouse slumbering history. I guess I hope that when it awakes it will tell me why towns like Barnsley struggle from one generation to the next to provide decent incomes for their hard-working citizens. If people really want to know why Brexit happened, all they have to do is visit Barnsley where all the accoutrements of civilisation have been worn away by the acid rain of austerity and globalisation. It has become like it was for me as a bairn when we became destitute and my dad had to beg the council to put him on poor relief. Having to ask for assistance to feed his children crushed my father's spirit like a submarine hull is pulverised by the weight of water if it goes too deep below the ocean's surface.

As poor relief was designed to be never enough to feed a family or keep a roof over your head, families like mine were always in arrears to either the landlord or the grocer. So, my mother pawning her wedding ring or her Sunday best was a habitual ritual, the same way modern families today who are too poor for credit tragically try to use pay-day lenders or modern pawn shops to keep their larders full or their bailiff from evicting them from overpriced, under-serviced flats.

Poor relief, like welfare benefits today, marked the recipient as a shirker, someone who didn't have enough self-respect to work. The shame of being compelled to ask for poor relief made my mother eternally angry at the state for humiliating our family for the crime of poverty.

The twelve-shillings-a-week poor relief was less than half a manual labourer's weekly pay in 1928. It guaranteed one thing: if you weren't cunning or lucky you would be dead in a year from malnutrition or despair. It's one of the reasons that my mum, even in later life, didn't think much of government institutions or their ability truly to help those in rough circumstances.

'That wretched Barnsley council,' she'd moan when she was an old woman, 'gave us poor relief but it wasn't enough to feed a family of bloody mice. Still, they made you feel when they gave it to you like they were Lord Mucks. You could see it in their eyes when they handed over pennies that they thought we were nowt but dirt.'

As we were near starving and penniless, my mum took to raising rabbits to try and make sure we had some meat in our diets. It was a failed enterprise because the local cats massacred them in their dilapidated hutches near our bog, which drove my mum berserk with rage. Over their bloody carcasses, she promised to anyone who was in hearing distance that she would hang every cat on the street in retribution for having our rabbits for their supper. It wasn't until my dad calmed her down by asking his old union to donate a buck and doe to help breed us a decent Sunday tea that the neighbourhood tabbies were safe from my mother's revenge.

At that time, my family was holding on to civilised life by a tender thread because we weren't able to keep our squat warm. In desperation, my mum enlisted my sister Alberta and me to forage for coal on the slag heaps that erupted like huge boils at the entrances of the coal mines that surrounded our slum. She handed us each a small bucket, kissed our foreheads and tried not to cry as she pushed us out the door 'to go find us some warmth'.

So, in the dull late afternoon light of October, my sister and I dug for refuse coal on a slag heap that towered above the colliery where my dad once used to labour until he was tossed from the employed world as if he was a broken piece of pipe. We were not alone on this mountain of pit waste because besides us and above us were other indigent children who dug, like their fathers once had beneath the ground, to keep the frost at bay in their homes.

Sewn into the mountain of rock, rubble and industrial waste were shards of coal that resembled splinters of wood, which my sister and I collected to be used in our fireplace at home. By the end of our scavenging, the soot had made my sister and me as black as canal water. We hauled our buckets of coal homeward and through the dusky teatime streets of Barnsley, where other bairns played by their clean stoops and looked at us as if we were wretched urchins. My sister, who was as brave as a lion, roared insults at them as we trod past while I, still very young, tagged along behind her bold shadow.

When we arrived home with our pails heaped high with chipped and rotten coal, my mother bit her lip and said,

'Look what the cat's dragged in.' With cold, brackish water, she scrubbed the dirt from my face and hands and then did the same to my sister, who fought her like a dog being dunked in bath water. No matter how hard my mother tried to clean me, there would always be a smudge left on my soul from the hunger, poverty and drudgery I'd already experienced by the age of five. After my sister and I had been cleaned up, my mother then dirtied my father's self-esteem by pointing out to him that, because he wasn't fit to do a man's work, his bairns were working like pit ponies.

I shudder and am angry when I remember what I had to do to keep warm. And nothing much has changed for Barnsley because there are 10,000 households today that are suffering from fuel poverty and they don't even have the ability to pick through the slag heaps in a desperate attempt to keep warm. All across this country, while energy company CEOs get fat on their bonuses, there are over 2.2 million households afflicted by fuel poverty. The raging greed of the big six energy companies that leaves Britain in the dark is fuelled by governments that have let them run riot with rising energy prices.

Moreover, the inability of many seniors or chronically ill people to afford the costs of heating their homes is a major factor in premature death because damp living quarters can exacerbate serious health conditions. In 2014, 31,000 elderly and vulnerable people perished during the winter months because fuel poverty caused serious ill effects to their health. It is no exaggeration to say that millions have a tough job of keeping the heat on in winter. I have aged relations in Bridlington, for instance, who basically live in their parlour with one electric heater to keep them warm until spring arrives since the price for heating their homes exceeds their pension incomes even with the winter fuel allowance.

It is a depressing thought but I see little difference between the heartlessness of today's Tories and the ones who ladled out, in teaspoons, poor relief to families like mine in the 1920s and 1930s.

Since the Tories came to office in 2010 they have viewed those in receipt of benefits because of illness or unemployment with the same measure of disdain as Britain's Prime Minister Stanley Baldwin did in the 1930s. Famously, Baldwin in 1936 refused to greet members of the Jarrow Crusade who were a collection of 200 men who had walked to London from the north-east of England to demand jobs for their region, which had experienced the collapse of its shipbuilding industry.

Simply put, if you are out of work in Tory Britain and do not have a skillset for a post-industrial society, the chances of finding a job that can cover your cost of living are slim to none.

The Department for Work and Pensions (DWP) has become a ministry that is more interested in bullying and castigating those made vulnerable by an economy in flux than providing comprehensive benefits programmes to assist both the unemployed and low-wage earners throughout Britain. It should alarm anyone to know that

David Cameron's government changed the in-work benefits scheme to penalise the working poor who are now being ground down like grain underneath a millstone because of this new legislation. These rules will punish individuals for not being able to work enough hours due to their zero-hour contracts, illness or the need to provide childcare to their infants, and will mean reduced financial support from the government.

It's simply horrific to see how the working poor are being traumatised by this government's new benefits programme that will make more people financially insecure and damaged by the cruelty of penury. This is especially true for those on benefits due to illness or disability, who have been brutalised by austerity and the sheer indifference of those like the former minister Iain Duncan Smith. In fact, the advocacy group Disabled People Against Cuts concluded that, between 2011 and 2014, 2,380 people died after their claims for benefits were denied as they were found 'fit for work'. Moreover, the changes to the Personal Independence Payment (PIP) have meant that some on disability living allowance are now being reassessed every year despite the fact that, for most, their impairments will worsen over time or become terminal. To be fair, Damian Green, who replaced Duncan Smith at the DWP, curbed some of the more excessive assessments for dying cancer patients that in the past found people deemed fit for work despite the fact that their life expectancy was no more than weeks. Green's empathy, however, is on a very short lead. In the lead-up to Christmas

2016, he declared that there would be no grace for those sanctioned for the simple transgression of showing up late to a job centre interview; a recipient's payments could be stopped during the holiday season, meaning a very cold and hungry Yuletide for some.

In my day, poor relief at best did little more than slightly increase the time it took to be pulled into a black hole of utter destitution. It's hard to see how the DWP's approach in the twenty-first century, with draconian sanctions and assessment testing that has been tendered out to private corporations like ATOS, is any better.

The humiliation that a recipient receives today through work assessment can be as painful as the means test my father underwent in 1928. When my family was assessed for poor relief, a government inspector pawed through our few scant possessions to determine if we were skint enough to warrant assistance. The visits of those inspectors to the rooms we occupied in Barnsley and Bradford stripped us of our dignity and made us feel ashamed of our possessions.

Thanks to Margaret Thatcher and David Cameron, desperate times just don't want to leave the north, and Barnsley is still wounded and bloodied by economic inequality that locks many families into generations of hopelessness on the dole or on low wages, just as it did in my boyhood. In fact, reports commissioned by Barnsley Central's Labour MP Dan Jarvis found that one-third of the children who inhabit his constituency exist in poverty because their parents can't afford to buy necessities.

That's why, even though I haven't lived in Barnsley for over eighty years, it still has a familiar feel to me when I visit. I can recognise the same hunger and want that afflicted my family decades ago. Fashions may have changed but not the look of despair on the faces of the people, who flit into pound shops looking for something affordable to buy for their tea. It's not right, it's not moral, it's not even logical that kids in Barnsley and elsewhere in Britain need food banks to keep them from suffering from malnutrition because their parents don't earn enough on zero-hour contracts or benefits to feed their offspring. You would think, after the billions that could be found to bail out the banks, that Britain would have the sense to maintain a social safety net that ensures every child in this country will get the required nutrients they need to develop both physically and emotionally into productive citizens. After all, governments in the 1950s, 1960s and 1970s put in place legislation that allowed all children free school meals and a milk allowance regardless of age or income so that no one would be stigmatised. To me, it seems almost unimaginable that, when London is the capital where the world stores its wealth and makes its greatest financial transactions, any child in our nation should be without a proper place to kip and a decent teatime meal.

The spirit of goodwill has always been alive in Barnsley and for that I am grateful. Without it, I would not have survived past my third birthday because I was kept alive by the trade union and community soup kitchens that were formed to feed the families of miners who had manned the pickets during the general strike of 1926. Today, that spirit can be found in the numerous food banks manned by volunteers that try to lend a hand to those who have been failed by this government.

Aside from the cars, little in my grandparents' street has changed over a hundred years. It's a living reminder of our ancestors who built this country but were never allowed to share in its wealth until the Atlee Labour government of 1945.

I walked away from my grandparents' living-room window and strolled through the ginnel beside the house that leads into the backyard. During summer, my grandmother could always be seen working her little patch of garden and flowerbed. I remember vividly the taste of the fresh strawberries and tomatoes that came from this garden when I was a hungry boy. I still remember the scent from her flowerbed, which produced roses of such exceptional colour.

Seeing the house, the backyard made me yearn to meet my grandparents again. I wish they could have lived long enough to see the birth of the welfare state that emancipated their grandchildren from the drudgery of hard physical labour without proper recompense.

I think both my granddad, who died of cancer in 1936, and my grandmother, who died of heart disease in 1946, would have strongly approved of the welfare state. After all, if it had been around when they were dying, they could have left this mortal coil in dignity rather than like wounded animals expiring in the woods.

I turned to leave and walk through the ginnel and touch its wall. I recalled how it steadied me when I first learned to ride a bike my Uncle Harold had lent me in 1930. On the road outside in 2016, I caught sight of a boy on a bike who disappeared down the hill. I smiled as I remembered the freedom I felt when I rode my uncle's bike to the countryside that once surrounded these houses and escaped the torment of my poverty in the ecstasy of a bright and warm summer's day in Yorkshire.

Still, things are a bit different from yesteryear in the town of my birth because, like many marginalised communities across our nation, there is tension between people of different faiths, races and culture, which wasn't as pronounced in my day. The industries that bound the people together and gave them a sense of pride have disappeared. Moreover, the new economy that emerged after Margaret Thatcher closed the pits and destroyed the miners' union didn't provide economically fulfilling work for all the inhabitants. Thatcher's destruction of the north and the failure of Labour governments to seriously address this created an underclass of people who lack the skills, the chances and the economic freedom to lead purposeful lives. There is no doubt that the pits were brutal places to work but the miners had a sense of pride in their hard toil that no job in this new sharing economy or the zero-hour-contract world has ever replaced.

That's why there is an angrier edge to people, which didn't exist in my youth, in all deprived regions of Britain today. It's evident that people are wise enough to know that a better life has been denied to them and they are growing angrier over the stagnation of their hopes because of austerity and globalisation.

I've found across the regions that I've visited that voted Brexit a profound disappointment by the inhabitants in what has been delivered to them in terms of schools, jobs and opportunities to succeed by both local government and Westminster. These citizens who live in cities or towns with crumbling infrastructure, hospital closures and pound-shop economies rightly feel cheated by politicians and businesses that never replaced good paying jobs once the factories were shuttered and the mines closed.

Globalisation and new technology have fractured communities and our society as a whole. While much of what I experienced in my youth is returning with virulence to my country, what is absent is the solidarity the working class had in my youth. We didn't have the internet, mobile phones or Twitter to corral our rage and also manipulate us with false information and anti-migrant propaganda. We understood our misery and, if we didn't know the cause of it, we had the good fortune of being educated about it by trade unionists, church groups, community activists and the Labour Party, who each told us that our misfortunes were the fault of the capitalistic system that was rigged to make the lives of the wealthy more comfortable. We were told that work only had dignity if it was fairly paid and that democracy could only work when all of its citizens shared in the prosperity of the nation through good schools and affordable housing. Today, those truths are drowned out by the raging voices of racists, fascists and right-wing business leaders who don't want a fair and equal society. I understand the anger of ordinary people. Hell, I felt it myself when I started full-time work at fourteen and saw other teenagers my age trundle off to school while I slaved away as a grocer's assistant because, coming from the working class, I was denied a higher education.

But what I don't get is why people today direct their animosity at the most vulnerable or people from different cultures. In the weeks that followed the EU referendum, reported hate crimes against minorities increased by 42 per cent. It is unsavoury that in this great and compassionate nation, since the referendum, Eastern European migrants have been stabbed and beaten in disturbing numbers by racist right-wing thugs.

I have seen this type of hatred before when I went to the cinema in the 1930s and watched Hitler ascend to power on a platform of hate for the vulnerable, hate for minorities, hate for Jews, hate for gays, hate for the infirm, hate for the Roma, hate for the outsider. That animosity towards others, then and now, leads humanity to genocide and wars that engulf all we hold dear.

That's why I am concerned how Brexit has emboldened racism in Britain. But we must remember that it wasn't the referendum that caused this rabid xenophobia but an economy that has removed the soul from places like Barnsley, Dewsbury and Rotherham. This rise in right-wing extremism exists because left-wing politics did not address the needs of those in the working class who were abandoned by neo-liberalism and globalisation. Identity politics is necessary but if we ignore the simple human need for people to feel that they can prosper in an economically chaotic time, we will always be under the thumb of conservative politicians. People like Nigel Farage and Theresa May will always manipulate us and never deliver on that basic human need to believe that our children will be better off than us until the left answers those questions, like they were answered in 1945 with a comprehensive plan for society.

The more Britain slips down the rabbit hole of Brexit, the harder it is to imagine that we will ever be able to preserve our NHS or maintain and improve our welfare state. It will take us years to try and establish trade deals that will keep our standard of living even at the current, unequal level.

It's why I thought, as I breathlessly walked away from my grandparents' old home, that if I could come back in another 100 years the despair would still smell as fresh on this street as a coat of paint put on the wall in the morning.

I stopped for a moment to catch my breath and thought of all the history that my family had experienced on this working-class street. It was here my mother was born and here she defied her parents' wishes by marrying my dad, who was much older than her. It was on this street that my uncles became socialists because of the 1926 general strike and the brutality the government showed to honest workers. It was here that I was taken when I grew ill from whooping cough just after my sister had died from TB because my parents didn't have any medication and believed my grandmother, with her knowledge of the ancient medical remedies of our class, could treat my sickness. It was here that, as a thirteen-year-old boy, I watched my granddad die in the living room because he was too weak to mount the stairs to sleep in his own bed. It was here that, when he died, I began to feel my spirit become politicised because I knew it wasn't right that he was denied pain relief in his final days because of poverty.

It was also here, at the time of his death, that my grandmother told me that I was Barnsley born and bred, and nowt, time nor brass could ever change my heritage. It was here that I also felt love and security that I rarely experienced during my childhood because of my parents' unemployment and financial destitution.

As I stood recalling that my own history was tethered to Barnsley, I closed my eyes and could hear my dad whistle a seaside melody while my heart beat excitedly at the thought of being with him on my way to market.

I trembled from these memories because all my images of him are precious and profound – my father disappeared from my life when I was the age of eight.

That's why my trip with him and my sister once long ago to the Saturday market was a profound journey. It was there that my dad treated us to mushy peas that were a penny a plate, and they were washed down with a shared bottle of dandelion and burdock pop. I'd dream on an empty stomach of that day we went to market when happiness could be bought for a penny.

Not long after that trip to the market with my dad, my grandfather took me and the rest of our family to the Remembrance Sunday service at the war memorial in Hoyland.

The air that day was thick with grief from all those who had come to pay respects to their sons, husbands, uncles and fathers who had taken the king's shilling and fallen in the Great War, which had only ended ten years previously.

On that long-ago Sunday, I don't remember whether the people wore poppies or not but the grief from that war was as fresh as a newly dug grave in a churchyard cemetery. Back then, symbols to remember the war dead weren't needed to prod the collective memory in the way they are today, for our citizens whose total experiences of war are limited to either endless bouts of *Call of Duty* on their Xbox or as viewers of television nostalgia that portrays early-twentieth-century Britain as steadfast, patriotic and stoic in the face of so much death.

So much time now separates us from the trenches of France that we understand little about the hardship and heartache of my parents and grandparents' generations. Over 38 million soldiers and civilians died in battlefields or on home fronts across the globe. Nearly three-quarters of a million British soldiers died in the Great War, some immediately from bullets, bayonets or gas on no-man's land. My granddad had sacrificed a son to that senseless war. His Tom, however, had died far away from the battle-fields of Europe in a seaside hospital in Scarborough. He perished at the age of twenty-two not from gas or a bayonet but from tuberculosis, which he contracted while in service in the Royal Army Veterinary Corps.

To his dying day, my granddad was only able to ease his sorrow over the death of one of his boys through an unbreakable faith in Britain. He convinced himself, like many have about Iraq, that lives had been sacrificed defending freedom and liberty. But there were a great many others, like my mum, who believed that their loved ones' lives had been squandered by an uncaring elite whose only concern was the preservation of their privileges, profits and position in an unjust society.

During that Remembrance Day service, I remember my granddad pointing at his son's name on the war memorial and saying, 'Never was and never will be a finer man than our Tom.' Years later, on returning to that memorial in the indifferent November rain, I once again found my uncle's name alongside the other lions who were led by donkeys, and I thought to myself that there is no one who was alive at the time left to weep for your passing or your gener-ation's wasted sacrifice.

Chapter Five:

Bradford and Poor Relief

Soon after that Remembrance Sunday service with my grandad, when the hurt from the loss of loved ones in the Great War was etched on people's faces like it had been cut with jagged glass, we left Barnsley forever.

My parents were exhausted from the misery of poor relief. Our survival as a family depended on us leaving this town and looking for better prospects in a larger place. So, we fled to Bradford in the dank days of late November 1928 in the hope that, within the limits of that city, there would be a factory, a mill or a shop willing to give my father a job that paid him enough to feed us all and provide lodging. My parents believed that nothing worse could befall them than what had already occurred in Barnsley.

The decision to lead us out of the wilderness was made by my mother because my dad's self-worth and confidence had been amputated from his character on the day he took poor relief. The shame of poverty fogged over my father's ability to know which way he needed to go to enable us to carry on as a family. I guess that's why he accepted without argument my mum's pronouncement that Bradford was our best chance of surviving the growing economic calamity in Yorkshire. 'There's real opportunity in a city that has jobs that don't require you to dig coal,' my mum told him and us, as if by wishing it she could make it true.

Besides, everything had turned sour for us in Barnsley after Marion died in the workhouse infirmary, and starvation or the workhouse were beckoning us too. In her retirement, my mum confessed to me that she 'never cried once over spilt milk. What's done is done. But I know that, had we stayed in Barnsley, all of us would have ended up dead like your sister.'

In the end, moving to Bradford didn't ease our troubles; it brought them to a head. Hope for work, for a change in fortune or for a chance that your children would get a decent life is what kept most poor families going in the 1920s and 1930s. It's what propelled us to leave Barnsley for Bradford – the belief that our luck could improve by changing our postal address. During those troubled years between the First and Second World Wars, when the mining, steel and shipbuilding communities were devastated by the Great Depression, thousands of people abandoned their neighbourhoods on a wing and a prayer. Some were lucky and survived the rising tide of unemployment and secured a job; others, like us and the vast majority of out-of-work Britain, were not.

This same type of optimism drives economic migrants today to faraway lands because human nature dictates that no matter the odds we will struggle to survive until the bitter end. But it is not just international migration. Regrettably, within Britain, not much has changed because similar economic pressures to those that forced my family to up sticks in 1928 still drive families to greener pastures in twenty-first-century Britain.

Each year, around 2.9 million people change regions within the borders of our nation, primarily for better work opportunities or to retire in less costly locations. We are the most migratory nation in Europe, which clearly indicates that all is not well with our economy. In fact, Britain has the highest level of income inequality for all G20 countries, according to studies conducted by Equality Trust UK. The divide between the haves and have-nots in Britain hasn't been this great since the 1930s.

The disproportion in wealth between the top 1 per cent and everyone else causes political tension, and the problem is worldwide. What touches Britain and the United States also touches the EU. Now there are enormous disparities in EU countries between the wages of their most skilled workers and least skilled workers because of the neo-liberalism that has curbed wage increases over the last two decades. Add in cutbacks to the social safety net and poorly designed integration of new immigrants, and it is only natural that political parties like the Front National in France and the Five Star Movement in Italy have gained prominence and escalated both nativism and demagoguery within their citizenry. The years 2016–17 across much of Europe felt more like 1938 before the storms of war swept across the globe.

I was made acutely aware of this when I visited the infamous and now disbanded Calais Jungle where thousands of refugees from wars in the Middle East and Africa congregated, in conditions I have not seen since the Second World War, in an effort to find a safe haven in Britain across the Channel. It confirmed to me that our Western world is sitting atop a funeral pyre built from the injustices of corporatism and arrogant greed. The match has been lit and a fire smoulders below our democracies.

The night before we left Barnsley, my family spent our last night in the town of my birth at my grandparents' overcrowded house. The next morning, my family said goodbye to our kin and walked to the bus station where we boarded a commuter bus that was bound for Bradford. I sat on an uncomfortable wooden seat between my mother and my sister, who complained for the entire journey about the unjustness of leaving Barnsley. My dad sat on the opposite side from us and held on his lap, as if it were a memento from a sunken luxury liner, the painting of my grandfather, which was wrapped in sack cloth.

My early experiences traipsing from one town in Yorkshire to the next as my family pursued steady employment make me grimace each time a spokesman from UKIP or the Tories talks about immigrants stealing British jobs or the evils of 'free' movement rather than attacking an economic system that benefits our richest corporations but makes people flee their homelands in search of better opportunities. Unless Britain wishes to become as xenophobic as Hungary or as racially biased as the USA, we must stop looking at the victims of neo-liberalism and globalisation as the impediment to a prosperous and well-rewarded life. In fact, the most dangerous threat to people's wages at the moment is Theresa May's promise to prioritise concerns people have on immigration over our need to belong to the single market, which means we are headed for a hard Brexit. This is incredibly dangerous for Britain because our nation may find, like in the 1930s, few willing to buy our goods because of the protectionist economics and nationalist politics of other nations, including the increasingly isolationist United States.

The political discourse Jeremy Corbyn has started in the Labour Party about the benefits of migration is good for this country. Corbyn believes that the real problem Britain faces isn't migration because newcomers to our country can add to its wealth through the valuable skills many bring here, through the taxes they pay and through the businesses they build. To Corbyn, the real issues that are destroying the prosperity of workers can be laid squarely at the feet of an establishment that encourages wage suppression, curtails the rights of trade unions, adopts the use of zero-hour contracts, pays a 'living wage' that no one can live on and dismantles many social services that people depend on. Naturally, Corbyn and Labour also understand that migration has affected marginalised communities that were gutted by austerity, which is why they have called for the Migrant Impacts Fund suspended by the Tories to be reinstated as it helped vulnerable areas shoulder the burden on services that can arise from an influx of low-skill migrants.

Considering that much of the Brexit vote was sold on a lie about migration and money spent on the EU, perhaps our best alternative is to go back whence we came rather than end up like the Donner party of pioneers who set out to cross America in 1846 for the promise of a better life in California, and ended up dead or lost and starving in the wilds.

I've seen the mob call out many times throughout my life that it's migrants that are ruining Britain. I remember the signs that said 'No Blacks. No Irish. No dogs' in both good times and bad. But we must remember what my generation learned in the 1930s: it's not migration that is eroding the fabric of our civil society but issues like low wages, lack of job protection, insufficient or too expensive housing, lack of opportunity and the state taking too little tax from either the elite or giant corporations. Our nation will never see a return to the great social gains my generation achieved after the Second World War until the debt the 1 per cent owes our society is settled through them paying a proper level of tax on their wealth.

Until that occurs, the poor, the jobless and the low wage earners will have few options except those my mother lived by: 'If the cards you're dealt are bad, best that you learn to bluff.' It's all she had. My mum used her charm and cunning or just talked bollocks to secure, before we left Barnsley, a roof over our heads in Bradford.

My mum struck a deal with a dodgy landlord to be his rent collector in a house that he'd overfilled with down-and-outers, on the condition that our rent for living there would be reduced. To get the bargain rent, the owner of the doss ordered my mum to give no quarter to anyone who was in arrears. Late in life, she said, 'I had no choice, lad, it were them or us for the chop. So, I don't regret putting people on the kerb because it's a miserable bloody world we live in.'

The doss was located in a derelict part of the city, on the site of what is now part of Bradford's university campus, so it took us a while to reach it on foot from the bus station. As we walked closer to our new location, the neighbour-hoods became more derelict and sinister.

I remember when I first saw the dosshouse; it frightened and beguiled me because it leaned precariously over the street like a ship listing in a storm. Each room in the doss was crammed with desperate families similar to ours or with Irish navvies who had come to Britain because Ireland was more famished than England. All of those people had ended up there because joblessness or age had left them unable to live in their previous accommodation. Simply put, both their money and luck had run out. So, they ended up having a very tenuous existence teetering over the pavement.

In today's Britain, with so many people only one payment away from mortgage default or eviction, there is no doubt that financial insecurity is just as prevalent. It is estimated that 16 million people of working age in this country have less than £100 in savings to tide them over in case of emergency. It is why, today for the jobless, the refugee and the disabled, the decaying holiday boarding houses found in neglected seaside towns have replaced the dosshouses of my youth for those sliding downwards on the ladder of life. The housing crisis is as pernicious as the one I faced as a boy. Five families every hour are made homeless in our country and many end up in places that are just as deplorable as where my family landed in Bradford. When over 100,000 children live in precarious housing such as other people's living rooms, B & Bs or temporary shelters, where entire families kip on the floor, we have to admit that David Cameron's Big Society and now Theresa May's shared society is more than a failure, it's a social catastrophe. Politicians have become like generals of old moving men to their doom as if they were chess pieces on a board. Like in my youth, we are nothing to the politician if we come from the wrong demographic: they only listen to those with money and pay to the declining middle class only lip service.

When we arrived in Bradford, my mum knew we had hit rock bottom and within her an urge grew that was stronger than empathy for others – to survive and ensure that her children emerged from this misery alive. She learned to hate and mistrust anyone who was not her kind.

'There's no second chances in this world, lad, and the only choice we have is to fight to stay-alive for as long as bloody possible because in the end something or someone will drag you down.'

Upon our arrival at our new home, my mother barged into the doss's common room, thick with shag tobacco smoke from a pipe being smoked by an Irish navvy enjoying his weekend day of rest. A half-dozen people sat on rotting furniture in dejected silence that was only broken by the sighs from a pregnant woman and the persistent coughs of a few weary pensioners in their last years. My mother Lillian announced in the voice of a drill sergeant that she was now in charge of collecting rents. My sister, my dad and I trailed behind her, like insignificant shadows, while she bellowed, 'There'll be no mucking about with me, thy rent will come on time or else I'll put you out on your ears, each and every one of you.'

At that moment, some in the room might have doubted the veracity of my mother's pledge to forcibly evict anyone who broke the rules because my mum was a slight woman who looked delicate. However, when she was crossed, her rage seemed to inflate her to the same proportions as a menacing beast.

It didn't take the tenants long to learn that my mum was good to her word. Within a few weeks of our arrival, her ire was raised by a young Irish lad who liked his beer but couldn't hold his bladder at night and habitually pissed his mattress. After complaints from others that his unwashed body and room had become offensive even to those whose luck, finances and personal hygiene were only one station above that of a tramp, my mother decided that the young navvy had to go immediately. She didn't hesitate when she saw him coming to the front door after he'd finished his shift at work. My mum screamed out his name and leapt up three flights of stairs like a raging fire burns through dry wood. My sister and I followed up behind her and watched as she pushed open the door to the navvy's lodgings, flung open his window and tossed the mattress and what little belongings he had to the pavement below. 'We'll have no piss-pants in this house,' she yelled down to the street while the humiliated navvy gathered his few possessions into a bundle under his arm. I remember watching him scatter from our doss like a cat that has been pushed with a broom and feeling both sympathy and relief that he would disappear into the wilds of Bradford.

The Irish lad may have been brutally turned out by my mum but it didn't rid the dosshouse of its foul stench. Rude odours lurked in its hallway. There was always the smell of thick sweat from both hard labour and lack of bathing facilities. It clung to the walls of the doss while the heavy smell of boiled cabbage and potatoes fried in lard wafted from the frying pans of the residents whose circumstances dictated that they cook the same meal, day in and day out. As for my family, our diet mainly consisted of dripping and fried bread washed down with weak tea that my mum called 'witch's piss'.

The menu may have changed for today's poor but not the circumstances that cause them to consume food that is low in nutritional value. Today, even though Britain is the fifth largest economy in the world, 8 million of our citizens are in various degrees of financial distress that prevents them from eating either regularly or nutritiously. In a twelve-month period in 2015–16, 16,000 people were admitted to hospital in England for malnutrition, 900 of whom were diagnosed by doctors as suffering from severe starvation, and 365 of whom died from hunger. Malnutrition accounted for 184,528 bed days that year, dramatically up from 2006–7 when it accounted for only 65,048. There is no question that diminished wages and benefit sanctions contributed to these people suffering a level of hunger that has not been seen in this country since my boyhood.

The problem today is the lack of availability of inexpensive, healthy food choices for marginalised people. There has been a rise in obesity in economically deprived areas throughout Britain as the poorer opt for cheaper, less nutritious food. In the government's 'Family Spending in the UK' survey for the year ending March 2016, it found that poorer families are forced to spend more of their disposable income on rent and heat: a low-income household spends 9 per cent of its income on heating, compared to 3 per cent for those on an average wage. People must remember that malnutrition in whatever form it takes isn't a lifestyle choice but a curse of poverty.

My mother might have been a rent collector but it didn't provide us with many privileges except cheaper lodgings. Our room was as dismal as any of the other occupants'. I remember going with my mother to the slumlord's house, situated in a posh part of Bradford, so that she could settle up with him. I was left to stand outside the front door while she did her business. In the window, I saw a boy my age practising the violin, which made me feel both envy and anger for the good life this lad was receiving out of our misery.

In fact, to me our Bradford abode was more miserable than the slums we had left in Barnsley. At least there, to my childish mind, I knew the neighbourhoods and had friends and family nearby. Here, there was nothing but dirt and fear of the unknown. Sometimes before I closed my eyes on the mattress I shared with my sister Alberta, I'd hear on the wooden stairwells the single beat of a peg leg from a one-legged soldier hobbling off to bed, which made me cry myself to sleep.

In my dreams, I'd see Barnsley and my grandparents but when I awoke, still dressed in my clothes with rags for blankets, my heart would sink. I knew that daytime was my real nightmare because each day began with my mother screeching at my father to find work.

As my mother bellowed at him, my dad would get up from his small mattress, which was only as thick as a Saturday newspaper. He'd stand demoralised and slowly walk over to our lone gaslight fixture that was attached to a wall painted in grime and ignite it with a long burning taper.

The light hissed and sputtered a weak yellow illumination across our stark room, where the light was never stronger than a dusky twilight. On a wall, close to the door, hung the painting of my grandfather. The eyes in the portrait seemed to stare back at us in bewilderment at how his progeny had sunk so low in life.

When we first arrived at this doss, I would cry in the morning because all we had for breakfast was some half-stale bread and tea that we drank from chipped jam jars. My father tried to give me comfort but my mother offered none except a warning or remonstration. 'Stop your crying,' she would bellow at me, 'there is nowt to wail about. You've got all your fingers and toes, so be thankful.'

After my father had left to search the city for itinerant labour, my mother set me to work helping her and Alberta scrub our room with a balding brush and bucket filled with weak soapy water.

While we cleaned, my mum intoned as it were a catechism, 'We may be poor but that doesn't mean we have to be dirty.' But we were filthy and our lives were muck-ridden because the house was infested with lice, vermin and the foul smells that emanated from the inhabitants who were so short of cash that even a trip to the local bath house was an unaffordable luxury.

As the house was full of navvies, our doss was always filled with drunken noises, fiddle playing and rough kindness from these men who toiled for pennies a day repairing roads or digging ditches. The young men flirted with my mother and she reciprocated their advances with banter, jokes and femininity.

My father, whose dignity had already been stolen from him when he lost his job in the mines, ignored her overt displays of affection to some of these men by smoking his pipe, reading his history of the ancient world or taking long walks alone.

As the weeks turned into months, my father still hadn't found work and my mother became more insulting to him in the company of others, especially the younger workmen who shared our digs. But during her storms of fury against his joblessness, he remained stoical and seemed to accept it as punishment for his inability to provide properly for us.

As my mum had little patience for him, he spent a great deal of his time talking to me about my ancestors who had been reared around Barnsley. He also loved to take me and Alberta to play in Lister Park, so that he could be out of earshot of my mum criticising him.

On those trips, he tried to imprint upon my soul his gentle sense of right and wrong by telling me tales about King Arthur, quoting Wordsworth or talking about his love for football. He also spoke to me of his time down in the pits. He liked to talk to me about when he first went down there as a boy of twelve, when the lamps were lit by candles and it was so dark it was like the Minotaur's cave. He would remind me that he had taken me once on to a picket line during the 1926 general strike. It was so that I would know that good men must always stand up against evil. 'Whatever you do in life, let no boss own your spirit.'

After our talks, he let me and my sister play 'King of the Castle' on the bollards that still dot Lister Park, while he sucked on a pipe that was bereft of tobacco.

But when we came home from those trips to the park, my mother would demand to know if he had looked for work. When he told her no, she'd scowl at him with a burning, accusative gaze that melted away any remaining pride.

In many ways, Barnsley, for me, is like Lake Victoria to the River Nile – all my triumphs and miseries flow from this one source. For us, our deprivation in Barnsley led directly to Bradford, my memories of which are splattered with scenes of horror, shame and anger. As a boy trapped in poverty living in one rank dosshouse after the next, I was tormented by nightmares. Each night I seemed to dream that I had the wings of a hawk and so could soar about this city that held so much anguish for its poor. In these dreams, I was always tricked into believing I could escape all my misfortunes by the beat of my wings, only to find that my leg was manacled to a chain that kept me tethered to a roof in a slum.

Even now, when I return as an old man, the air in Bradford always smells to me of dreams turned to cinders by the scorched-earth policies of austerity that afflicted this city in the 1930s and today. In 2017, life is not good for the desperate and vulnerable in Bradford; thanks to Tory policies of austerity, the city has levels of childhood poverty that are above the national average in all of its constituencies and that is unconscionable in twenty-first-century Britain.

Bradford and Poor Relief

Every time I go back down south to London, I am reminded that not much has changed in regional economic disparities since my youth. The Home Counties enjoy an abundance of wealth, while the rest of the nation makes do on reduced services and fewer well-paid jobs.

It's why any time I walk near the Kirkgate Shopping Centre in Bradford, while impecunious crowds weighed down by personal debt and the tyranny of zero-hour contracts bustle by me to find a bite to eat on their way home from work, I feel the same loneliness I had as a boy strolling these streets hungry and alone. Bradford is still haemorrhaging from economic inequality. It is a town littered with pawn shops, pay-day lenders, bingo halls and desperation. The city's poor still rely upon the St Vincent de Paul Society that provided me with filthy corduroy trousers in 1930 so that I could attend school. I can still hear the teasing words thrown at me like stones by children who were fortunate enough to have a parent in employment and had contempt for my sorry state.

What happened to me and my family in Bradford is still in my marrow despite the years that separate me from it. So, it enrages me that bairns born in this new century experienced the sufferings I encountered in this city during the dark ages of the Great Depression. It cannot change unless these new generations show the courage of mine and demand more from their lives than pay-day loans and zero-hour contracts.

When I walk these streets, I think of my father who trod these pavements looking for work. He found no employment or helping hand. And the question now is, after seven years of austerity, is it any different today for young parents looking to protect their children from the stark sadness of poverty? It is not and the reason why is because each time a citizen ignores their duty to vote in either local or national elections for progressive political candidates, they are helping to usher in a new epoch of ideologically driven poverty.

It has always amazed me that despite all the humiliations my father received because of being jobless, he never lost his humanity or became hard hearted, unlike my mother. Even when our situation was at its worst, my dad insisted on treating me for my sixth birthday by taking me to the Alhambra theatre.

I still wonder how he scraped the pennies together to take me to watch a pantomime of *Humpty Dumpty* in February 1929. It was a magical time, despite the fact that we sat in seats as distant from the stage as our dosshouse was from heaven. Our view was obscured by a support beam but nothing diminished my joy that day. When my father disappeared from my life at the age of eight, I used to return as many times as possible to stand outside the Alhambra. I'd stare at the people queuing for performances in the hope that I would catch sight of my dad. But he was long gone because the Great Depression had devoured him.

Not long after my birthday trip, the stock market crashed, which heralded the beginning of the Great Depression. Tens of millions of workers across the globe were now placed into the economic position my family had known since the general strike of 1926. After the stock-market crash, Bradford dissolved into a city of abject destitution as tens of thousands of working-class people were thrown out of work in the city's mills.

At first, my parents took comfort in the fact that Britain was being governed by a Labour government. 'It won't be that bad or long with Ramsay MacDonald at the helm,' said my dad to my mum one night in the common room. My parents, my aunts, my uncles, my grandparents and all the residents in the doss believed that voting for Labour had been their insurance policy, which they thought would save them from the deluge. However, Prime Minister MacDonald didn't save them and soon enough my parents realised they had been cheated.

MacDonald's method of handling the Great Depression in 1929 was as disastrous as George Osborne's solution to end our Great Recession caused by the 2008 financial crash. He, like Osborne, introduced spending cuts and austerity and, in a nation without any real system of benefits and protection for ordinary people, it was murderous.

The suffering that Labour's first prime minister unleashed earned my mother's long-term distrust for the party. 'Aye, they talk a good game but when it came to helping us the common folk, when we were starving, they did nowt. I voted for that bugger and I didn't put my X on another ruddy piece of paper for sixteen years because of what a so-called man of the people did to the people.' In 1945, my mother at the age of fifty cast a ballot for her first time since

1929 because now, she said, 'It's time to dump the rubbish into the tip.'

Most in the working class came to despise Ramsay MacDonald. They hated him the way some hated New Labour for leading us into the Iraq War in 2003 and today loathe them for abstaining on David Cameron's Welfare Reform and Work Bill.

During the 2016 battles between the Constituency Labour Parties and the Parliamentary Labour Party over whether Jeremy Corbyn should remain as leader, I thought a lot about how my mother never forgave Labour or Ramsay MacDonald for imposing austerity and splitting the party in 1931. Whatever Labour did to improve her lot following 1945, and it was plenty, she never believed that she had been fully recompensed for what she and her children endured during the Great Depression. I fear that many people today will think the same of those in New Labour who sought to discredit and remove Jeremy Corbyn with a desire spurred by nothing more than pollsters and the words of political cynics. Had the Parliamentary Labour Party been victorious in their coup against Corbyn, the 2017 general election could well have seen a Tory majority because their appointed leader would have been seen as just another side of neoliberalism.

My parents' politics were simple; they believed that they were owed something more than a wage, more than poor relief, for being human beings. They believed they were owed the right to dignity and the ability to lead a life that was free of want. It was a dream that was never realised for them because my father died long before the welfare state and my mum's spirit died in the slums of Bradford even though she lived well into her eighties.

It amazes me that most people didn't develop my mother's cynicism to politics in the 1930s. Throughout all the infighting and divisions that Labour endured during that decade, 72 per cent of the population religiously voted in the 1929, 1931 and 1936 elections. Today, except for the EU referendum, which saw a strong voter turnout, only around 65 per cent of eligible citizens vote, which means that 35 per cent of voters think democratic indifference is the solution to their economic and social problems.

Perhaps the reasons why people don't vote today are the same as my mum's; she believed her issues were too immediate to ever be solved by the 'Lord Mucks of London'. But the only way to change our country is to vote within the system we have now, and also demand that proportional representation be implemented along with a law making it mandatory for all citizens to vote or at least cast a spoiled ballot.

Chapter Six:
Childhood of Hunger

In January, as the door to 1930 opened, a coffin lid built from animosity, lack of communication and frustration was closing down upon my parents' marriage. Their relationship just couldn't withstand the pressure from our crumbling fortunes.

It was inevitable, I suppose, that my parents' marriage failed because their affection just couldn't survive the growing economic crisis caused by the crash of 1929. Financial doom rode across Britain like the horsemen of the Apocalypse and few were spared the wrath caused by governmental indifference to either joblessness or the flood tide of poverty, which submerged many regions that had once prided themselves on their industrial might.

My mother was mentally oppressed by the damage the Great Depression was doing to her family and herself. It caused her to suffer from severe panic attacks that plagued her for the rest of her life. There is no doubt in my mind that my mum's anxiety was produced from the stress of having to measure out a bread ration for her children of two slices per day during the worst moments of the economic crisis. She was transformed into a misanthrope who had no trust in politics, society or even ordinary people. 'The moment the food ran out,' she said of the 1930s, 'we all turned into dogs.'

My family felt the sting of the Great Depression quicker than most because we were already laid low. It made us like passengers in steerage on the *Titanic* when it struck the iceberg; we were the first to feel the destructive force of a ruptured economy and we knew our chances of emerging unscathed were slight. This economic havoc was destroying everything and everyone who didn't have employment or if their work was tenuous, like someone today on a zero-hour contract. I remember seeing people in their sixties arrive at the doorstep of our doss trying to rent a room on the cheap. Every one of them looked shattered; neither their mind nor their spirit could account for how they had been turned into paupers by the machinations of financiers and an indifferent government in London. It was this same type of despair in Britain's deprived areas that drove people into the arms of Brexit in 2016. When there is no hope, people, if given false optimism by a demagogue, will choose the devil they don't know.

When unemployment surged above 16 per cent during that first calendar year of the Great Depression, it created dread in those newly let go and terror in those still earning a wage because redundancy was just a footfall away – their time to be hungry was nigh, which meant panic was now in each breath taken by the working class. Britain was very lucky then that those who had fallen on desperate times did not fall under the sway of a political pied piper like Nigel Farage.

Although horribly damaged by the Great Depression, people of my parents' generation and mine had enough common sense to know when they were being utterly deceived by the likes of Oswald Mosley. The sentiments of hate against the outsider in the 1930s drove the people of continental Europe into the arms of fascists and right-wing extremists. In Britain, thankfully, when Mosley and his blackshirt British Union of Fascists tried to encourage the working class to become adherents of Nazism, few listened. At Mosley's height of popularity, his BUF had 50,000 members whereas the Labour Party in the 1930s had several hundred thousand members. But we must never forget that while the working class didn't fall under the allure of fascism, many in the aristocracy did, including the Duke of Windsor, who became an admirer of Adolf Hitler and his strongman politics.

Today, with similar problems arising, many of the working class seem to have lost the instincts that were able to detect not only danger but political cobblers. This is leading us into the cul de sac of Brexit and it seems that no one in Westminster has the gravitas to stop our plunge over the cliff as if we were sheep being herded by a mad dog.

In the 1930s it was different; we understood the system was rotten and we knew those at the top were the culprits for our misfortune, but hunger weakened our ability to fight back.

During the darkest period of the Great Depression, 25 per cent of our population's daily intake of calories fell far short of what was required to maintain one's health. We were on the verge of a national famine. However, in regions like the north or Scotland the percentage of those who were suffering from extreme food shortages caused by unemployment were much higher. Malnutrition was so widespread among the working class that during the call-up of troops in the Second World War, the government was informed that many who had enlisted were below the required weight and height for a good fighting soldier. When I joined the RAF in 1941, a friendly sergeant major told me that I needed to be fattened up for slaughter because 'dripping wet, you're just skin and bloody bone'.

When I was a thirteen-year-old in 1936, there was nothing that stank more of hypocrisy than when Edward VIII said 'something must be done' after visiting a Welsh coal-mining community that had been devastated by intense and unrelenting poverty. 'He's as rich as bleeding Croesus,' said my Uncle Ted to me. 'If he really wanted to help, he'd open up his wallet and shut his flipping mouth.'

Whether it's a dead king or the present prime minister, words of solicitude to the common people are like candle smoke that floats on the air for a brief moment and then it is gone. All of David Cameron's words, pledges and decrees on ending childhood poverty signified nothing because they were the gestures of an empty and hollow opportunist. In 2010, he came to Downing Street and pledged to defeat childhood poverty but when he left office in June 2016 there were 224,000 more children in poverty than before he made that mellifluous promise to the nation. And Theresa May, whose moral compass is permanently polarised by the needs of corporate Britain over ordinary Britain, doesn't even bother to pay lip service to the blight of childhood poverty. Her government's solution to ending childhood poverty is to close the Child Poverty Unit, created by Tony Blair, which had a proven track record of reducing childhood poverty.

The only way you can ensure that a government keeps its promises to you is if you are rich, which is why Chancellor Philip Hammond made sure to protect his predecessor George Osborne's commitment to big business to cut corporate taxes in his 2016 autumn statement, despite the uncertainties caused by an impending Brexit.

Today's Tories are no better or worse than the ones who abused my generation in the 1930s with their belief that indigence was a moral failure rather than a flaw in society.

Damian Green, the Work and Pensions Secretary, is a prime example of a Tory who has become a prisoner to his economic priggishness. Green can't stop talking in Parliament or to the press about the benefits to one's self-esteem work brings for the mentally ill, without addressing the simple fact that many people's mental illnesses are so profound that to ask them to put in a forty-hour week is like asking a stage-three liver cancer patient on chemo to do the same.

*

For the most part, the hard-pressed have always been cheated by politicians and their politics of compromise that always weigh in favour of those with wealth rather than those without. It means if you want to make serious changes to society the best way is to join the political party that you feel best exemplifies your outlook and work at the grassroots level to make sure politicians keep their word. Perhaps if we'd been able to hold the soles of our politicians' feet to the fire in the 1930s, that decade wouldn't have been as great a tragedy for people like my mum.

I have no doubt that a great deal of drug and alcohol dependence today is produced by either the stress of keeping oneself afloat in austere times or the emotional and mental discomfort that unrelenting poverty produces in those who have nothing. It's why so many people throw themselves into the self-defeating opium of reality TV and fake news: they divert the mind from the sheer devastation that is going on in their soul.

Sadly, mental illness produced by poverty or at the very least exacerbated by it is on the rise in modern Britain. Studies by poverty.org have concluded that individuals who comprise the poorest fifth of society are 24 per cent more likely than a more affluent group to suffer from some form of mental illness. Manual workers are more prone to depression, which can be linked to both their income and the precariousness of their work. That the Treasury has predicted low-wage workers are set to lose £800 per year once

Brexit has been ratified is troubling for the mental state of the British working class. It is unconscionable that, because of the political cynicism of politicians like Michael Gove, Boris Johnson and Nigel Farage, Britain will leave the EU without proper protection for ordinary workers. Our departure from the EU will not only affect the pocket books of the working class but the emotional wellbeing of those individuals who are already struggling financially.

I know my father must have suffered enormous torments because of the collapsing economy, but, as was the custom of that era, he tried to hide it from everyone. In many ways, however, his dismay over our slide into destitution couldn't be concealed. Some under duress will take to drink or rage but my dad did neither; he just emotionally withdrew from us like light at the end of a winter's day.

In his need to earn a wage once again, my dad tried everything and anything. He even took me and my sister with him to the front gates of the Weetabix plant in Bradford in the hope that our pathetic appearance would help land him a job. My dad was so desperate for work that he held me aloft at the front of the factory's wrought iron gate. In the blustery wind of a midwinter morning, he called out to the work supervisors nearby to beg for a job, only to receive the curt reply, 'Sorry, mate.'

Today, unemployment is at a record low but not tenuous employment, which has been caused by our so-called gig economy that has changed the nature of work and the relationship between employer and employee.

There are now over a million individuals who have licensed themselves as a small business. It is not because these people suddenly became entrepreneurial and turned into the Lord Sugars of their tenement neighbourhoods. No, it is because the only way their employers would hire them was if they first registered as a business. The reasoning of these employers is as simple as it is avaricious: when their employees are treated as individual businesses neither proper wages nor benefits are required for the contracted individual. When someone on a zero-hour contract who works at Sports Direct is considered a business, you know the system is being gamed to make the Mike Ashleys of this world extremely wealthy. This new service economy is just as bad in many ways as the jobless world my father faced. People might not be standing in front of the factory gates looking for a bit of work; instead, they are sieving social media for jobs that pay less than the minimum wage and have no permanence. I can't help but feel great anguish for today's young because they share the pain my father knew when he worked but could not make a living.

It's sad for me to relive the emotions as we walked away from those factory gates on that day long ago. He held me tightly in one hand and my sister in the other. The grief of failure radiated through his palms to me. I guess it dawned on him that he would always be down and out until the day he died.

It was an agonising walk home for him because he knew what awaited him at the doss – our mother's infernal rage. And it was so, because upon our return, when my dad told my mum for the hundredth time that there was no work going for tinker, tailor or soldier, she fell upon him like a dog made angry by cruel teasing. I remember him standing silent and defenceless against my mum's words as they rained down like a shower of bullets.

As the months progressed from the stock-exchange crash of October 1929, proud men who had once manned the lathes, looms and lorries that kept Britain's economy strong were let go and shop floors across the country grew quiet. As if they were soldiers defeated in a horrendous battle, men who used to punch a clock shuffled shell-shocked through the streets of our nation looking for work and hoping that the government had a plan to return them to gainful employment. But they were doomed because, as winter blossomed into spring, a million men were now on the dole – each of them trying to claw their way out of the poverty unemployment produced.

Persistent hunger and the prospect of death for both me and my sister gnawed at my mother's love for my father. She was starting to believe that her loyalty to my dad was driving us to extinction. From that point on, my mum began to follow her own set of laws and morals.

As the Great Depression's grip on Bradford and Britain became more formidable, she became like an animal caught in a trap that then tries to gnaw off its own limb to escape. She began to disappear for hours from our room only to return late in the night with the loudness of someone who has drunk too much. My father would demand to know where she had been, only to be rebuked for his unemployment. After each brief and bitter argument, Mum would slip under the pair of dirty coats my parents used as blankets and fall off to sleep after angrily cursing my dad, God and anyone who had crossed her path that day. My sister and I slept huddled together under our own jackets and coats for warmth, dreading the arrival of day.

By sunrise, my parents were always in a state of belligerence and rows of extreme animosity were the norm. If my mum noticed that my sister and I were awake, she'd break away from hectoring our dad to say with bitterness, 'There's nowt for your breakfast again because your dad can't find work. Try the Allens downstairs to see if they can lend you both a piece of bread.' Whereupon my sister Alberta would say something sarcastic to our mother and then hurry me to put on my jacket.

In the brittle Bradford air before school, I hunted for food with my sister to give us the energy to make it through the day. We weren't alone in this pursuit; the city teemed with street urchins who had grown feral because of the Great Depression. Sometimes, we'd return to the Weetabix factory and beg for cereal from the wagon drivers. Many ignored us and looked the other way so as not to see the desperation on the faces of us kids who plaintively begged for food. However, there were a few wagon drivers who showed some human compassion, and a rag-and-bone man also befriended me. He, with a face darkened from decades of unwashed grime, let me share his breakfast of a boiled egg on occasion.

An empty belly will drive you like a wild animal to do anything to satiate that hunger. In the United States, there have been numerous reports since the crash of 2008–9 of young teenagers as well as migrant workers who must sell their bodies to unscrupulous and evil people for a decent meal. Despite Barack Obama's grand words about a better society, most social programmes were either eliminated or scaled back by him and the Republican-controlled Senate. Moreover, now that Donald Trump is president there is no doubt that poverty among children will increase to levels not seen since the Dust Bowl years of the 1930s, which will cause an acceleration of racial tension and civil strife.

When I was at my hungriest as a boy, I would have done anything for a good cut of meat on my plate. Sometimes, the intensity of my hunger drove me to troll the city's back alleys with my sister before school. I'd dive into the skips and rubbish bins of Bradford's restaurants like a cat wrestles through waste to find a half-eaten fish, but I was no feline – just a boy of seven whose malnutrition had turned him so wild that he didn't think twice about eating the scrapings from an employed man's plate that he had pushed away the night before because his stomach was full.

We were the abandoned generation and I fear that the same is happening to my grandchildren's generation by the sheer short-sightedness and greed of those who hold seats in Parliament.

Theresa May claims her decisions are influenced by her belief in God, but unless this is the god of Mammon, it is hard to see how failing to tackle childhood poverty, appeasing Donald Trump's racism or selling fighter aircraft to Turkey's strongman Racep Tayyip Erdoğan has anything to do with Christianity.

My hunger for food and for social justice ended on the day Clement Attlee was elected Prime Minister in 1945. The 1945–51 Labour government made a lasting mark on Britain but that mark is now fading because of a change in the political direction of this country. Hunger is back with a vengeance because we've forgotten our democratic heritage that was committed to freeing us from want, ignorance and poor health.

It is not only wrong but dangerous for our society when 3.9 million Britons must go without meals to ensure that their children receive proper nutrients or that their rent can be paid on time. Hunger, homelessness and hopelessness are the matches that start the blaze that will burn down societies. Brexit and Trump are just the start of civilisation's spiral downwards unless we tame capitalism like my generation did to build the welfare state.

We should as a nation be ashamed that, in 2015, over a half-million families required a three-day emergency supply of food from the Trussell Trust to see them through tough times created by government-induced austerity.

Right now, because of the epidemic of low-income work and zero-hour contracts, an army of employed people are forced to survive on the charity of food banks to supplement their diets or queue at modern-day soup kitchens for their tea. That people in their thousands have become reliant on soup kitchens in 2017 doesn't indicate to me that society is showing its humanity, but rather that the greed of the top earners has left society as broken as it was in the 1930s. No one in work or out of work in twenty-first-century Britain should have to use a food bank but Tory austerity has normalised their use as if this is the solution to hard times. The misery of millions looms on the horizon and that's why my memories of Britain's past economic struggles constantly prick me. All it takes is to feel the sun or the rain on my face as I walk near Bradford's ornate Victorian town hall and a myriad of images begin to attack my imagination like chicks pecking at a sickly bird.

In my senior years, Bradford can look benign and welcoming but that is because I draw an old-age pension and have found modest comfort in my autumn years. But what a forbidding place the council offices here must have been for people like my mother and father when they came here to ask for relief during the Great Depression. My parents' cries of anguish over the hunger of their children and their stunted lives are now still; time has erased their suffering from the landscape of Bradford. It's all been forgotten but new miseries have grown from the shoots of old ones. Mothers are still trying to make ends meet on today's benefits and begging for help from overwhelmed council workers.

Childhood of Hunger

This is a city as divided by wealth as it was when I dug through rubbish looking for my tea. Poverty still lingers and haunts the streets of my youth and shortens the lives of many in this great city. Too many are still in need of affordable housing but this is not unique to Bradford – it is as ubiquitous as the rain because every town and city in our nation aches from austerity. None of this will change as long as governments in London listen to the siren song of hedge funds and the wealthy who fight our nation's need for more tax revenues from our most affluent citizens and corporations. Selling off council housing is not the answer to the housing crisis; raising tuition fees is not the answer to our education crisis; and terminating the grant for nursing students is not a balm for the NHS staffing crisis. Each of those remedies has more to do with the mindset and myopia of the 1 per cent than a correct cure for what ails Britain.

When my generation built the welfare state, we didn't eliminate wealth: we tamed it and harnessed its energy through taxation and nationalisation schemes. The welfare state erected by the 1945 Labour government was a sturdily built shelter that kept out inclement economic weather. In fact, it was so strong that successive governments, including Tory ones, built upon Labour's success.

It certainly eliminated hunger, extended our life spans, made us more educated and gave us a chance to enjoy moments of leisure denied to my parents and grandparents' generations. But that is all gone now and not because socialism failed Britain or, as Margaret Thatcher infamously said, socialism was all right until it ran out of other people's money. No, it's all gone because the children of my generation forgot the struggle of their parents or grandparents and allowed corporations to assume the roles and duties of the state. For the past thirty years, both Labour and Tory governments have been too enamoured by the majesty of corporate power and excess to comprehend that, to create a just society, you must tame the beast of capitalism, not let it roam free like a rampaging beast.

All people really want in this world is a chance to make good on their lives through the opportunities that affordable healthcare, education and decent paying jobs provide. The only way that is obtainable to the majority is through a welfare state that is not only compassionate but progressive in its mandate to lift people out of unhappy and unproductive circumstances.

Chapter Seven:
The Unravelling of Love and Loyalty

In 1930, my parents' love and respect for each other slipped its moorings. After the tragedies of the First World War, my sister Marion's hard death from spinal tuberculosis, the famine caused by the 1926 general strike and my father's loss of his job in the mines from an industrial accident, the long dark night of economic eclipse that followed afterwards proved too much for my mum and dad to handle as a loving couple.

My parents' marriage didn't end like it would today through either mutual agreement or bitterness followed by a court ruling; it ended in secret. There was no divorce. Nonetheless, there was termination and it finished with acrimony. Moreover, it ended in shame for both parties because back then it was a man's world and no woman, especially a working-class woman, was supposed to question the hierarchy of the universe by walking away from a marriage, like my mum did.

In the end, it was infidelity that finished my parents' marriage but, in truth, their love had been betrayed by an economy that wasn't prepared to give working people an honest break. I suppose I was the first to know that my parents' marriage was over but I didn't realise it at the time. I caught my mum coming from the room of a young navvy who lived in the same doss as us.

It wasn't unusual for my mum to be in the rooms of the other guests because she collected the rent. What was unusual, however, was how she looked and reacted when she left this man's digs. She emerged with a flushed face and her dress askew. I remember she adjusted her hair as if it were morning just before breakfast, instead of late afternoon. At first, my mother didn't see me staring at her but when she did there was a look of irritated fright. Then she came to me and said, 'Not a word to your dad,' which filled my heart with foreboding.

I understand now because I am very old why my mother left my father and why she had affairs with some brutal men who weren't kind to her and used her terribly. It was simple: my mother had few skills or assets to barter for our survival except her sex appeal. Mum began to use it in a desperate bid to initiate a relationship with an employed man – one who could carry the load for an entire family. All she wanted was a man who had work to keep us from sinking further into the quicksand of poverty. We were desperate and she understood that, in the rough-and-ready world we lived in, nothing was sacred because neither love nor loyalty would put bread into her children's hungry bellies.

For those reasons as well as simple loneliness, she began an affair with a navvy, who was named O'Sullivan. He was quick with the gab and thought of himself as a ladies' man and my mum fell prey to his charms.

Somehow, my mum believed it was her only way of emerging intact from the chaos wrought by the Great Depression. But it was a brutal choice to make because it marked her even to her own kin as a fallen woman. And, from the moment she left my father's bed to take up with other men for food, security and a roof over our heads, she was judged harshly by everyone including me and my sister Alberta. Perhaps the only one who didn't judge her so severely was my dad. He had come to accept that he must be sacrificed so that his children could live and in due time, like Captain Oates in the Antarctic, he would leave our doss to perish alone.

As 1930 progressed, the nation's output from its industrial centres in the north of England, Scotland and Wales shrivelled like the flow of a river during a time of drought because demand diminished for goods across the world as more and more people lost their jobs. By 1933, our world trade output had fallen by half and the output by heavy industry was down a third. We were no longer a great nation of industry or commerce but a wounded beast that had dragged itself into the forest to either heal or die. The great industrial collapse of the Great Depression was also caused by protectionist policies imposed by the United States and other countries.

Every time I hear Donald Trump threaten to tear up the North American Free Trade Agreement, while Theresa May tries to woo him with a trade deal that will ultimately betray the working people of Britain, I can't help but think of the breadlines of my youth. Should we leave the EU because of Brexit in 2019, we are going down a path that leads directly to my front doorstep eighty years ago in doss-infested Bradford. Not even Hitler's war against our island was as devastating as mass unemployment to our citizens in the 1930s because it cut the slender threads that made society civilised and humans decent. The government could have eased the misery by investing in infrastructure projects that would require mass employment like Franklin D. Roosevelt did with his New Deal in 1933. But instead they chose to pay down our war debt and hoped the malaise would be brief. However, the Great Depression wasn't short-lived and in some form or another its brutality lasted for most of the decade and only the mobilisation for war brought our nation back to full employment.

In that desperate time, most of the inhabitants of Bradford and any other city in Britain were as doomed as struggling citizens are today in many Third World countries. Wealth in 1930s Britain, like today, was concentrated in too few hands and the wealthy in government, on the boards of the mighty or running the media. The same is happening today when the right-wing tabloids attack those on benefits or deride the worsening refugee crisis as a scam filled with unscrupulous economic migrants out for a free ride, and the government wrings its hands and says the welfare budget is bankrupting the nation. These words come from politicians or tabloid editorials because they believe in maintaining the riches of the 1 per cent, and that can only happen through an adherence to low taxation of our rich citizens and companies.

Too many in the middle class have lost their capacity to be outraged about real injustice. Their voices have grown quiet when it comes to wage inequality, unless they can point the finger at the migrant. They are schtum when it comes to the housing crisis unless they can blame the migrant for making affordable housing out of the reach of millions. They are mute when it comes to workers' rights and prefer to blame the 'tyranny of the union bosses'. But silence only breeds contempt in the elites who govern us. To end job losses and low wages, our citizens have to stop taking the bait set by right-wing publications or by political parties like UKIP and the Tories. Ordinary citizens must begin to realise that the only protection for workers or managers will come when trade unionism can expand their reach into the new zero-hour economy as well as our old industries.

I saw during the Great Depression this same indifference from the middle classes who, if they caught children like me riffling through rubbish bins, chased us off instead of providing us with a hot meal. Today, many of us normalise poverty by stepping around homeless people on the street without giving them even a moment's thought. I have relatives in their late twenties who think people in need of state assistance are just alcoholics; one even told me at a Christmas gathering several years ago, 'You know, it's hard to feel sympathy for them when you see they are queuing up at the off licence before 10 a.m. in the morning.' They forget that their direct ancestors were thought of by the middle class in the 1930s as layabouts, drunks and charlatans for needing poor relief.

Xenophobia and bigotry always increase during uncertain economic times because racists and right-wing elements in government and society know they can divide us through spreading hateful falsehoods about minorities. Too many people in this country view the worsening refugee crisis that is overwhelming Europe as something that we should stay well away from, and excuse their callousness by claiming that those who arrive on Europe's shores are not authentic like those in the 1930s who fled Hitler's Germany. The sad irony is that the middle classes in Britain in the 1930s, abetted by tabloids like the *Daily Mail* portraying Jews as vermin or communists intent on destabilising our way of life, used that same excuse to turn their back on refugees who were subsequently gassed in the Holocaust. The tactics used by UKIP, and unfortunately now large swaths of the Conservative Party, to portray Muslim refugees as either terrorists or welfare scroungers are little different from what was employed in the 1930s against Jewish refugees. When people wince at my comparison, they generally say refugees aren't facing extermination like they were during the Nazi period, but there are valid comparisons to be made, not least because many refugees have faced threat to their lives.

Yet we persist in denying refugees sanctuary. A poll conducted by the Pew Research Center concluded that 52 per cent of British citizens view refugees entering our country as a grave threat to our economy, our society and our national identity. The negative propaganda and the fake news that has maligned Muslims and refugees initially allowed President Trump to execute an order barring all refugees, travellers and immigrants from seven countries based upon their religion. No Western democracy since the days of Adolf Hitler has ever introduced a more draconian and fascist measure and this has happened because the United States is in thrall to neo-liberalism. Whether this ugly politics will further push the boundaries of decency and democracy is uncertain but it is clear to me that our societies have been hijacked by the malevolence of wealth without morality.

It is not just the outsider who is at risk of being castigated by our rabid right-wing press. Years of propaganda by tax-avoiding media conglomerates has poisoned the British people against their own kind who are less fortunate. No longer do they see the poor or the unfortunate as part of the same human species as them but as a scourge, which is why councils from Oxford to Newport have attempted to pass legislation to ban the homeless from their city limits. Manchester has even barred them from public libraries because they upset middle-class patrons who don't want to be confronted by the ugliness of austerity. Had libraries banned the homeless, the dirty, the mentally ill and the socially outcast from their buildings in the 1930s, I would have been denied my right as a human being to explore the history, the culture and the literature of my nation. It is a sad indictment on our society if a human being's value to their community is judged solely by their ability to afford school fees, trips to the south in winter and private health insurance.

It is also disturbing to comprehend that 42 per cent of the electorate think immigration is the hot-button issue when, in fact, it should be the injustice and the rank pornography of entitlement. We have to face facts: it is not the Polish migrant workers at Lidl that are upsetting the balance of society but the fact that 10 per cent of the richest households in this country own 45 per cent of Britain's wealth. The only possible reason why people can believe it is immigration that threatens us is not ignorance but political and ideological indoctrination that is injected into society through a right-wing media with questionable motives and ethics. Moreover, our Tory government is using the same tactics employed by politicians during the 1930s to deflect from their glaring failure to address declining wages, crumbling social services and infrastructure, which has left millions destitute.

If Britain is to survive as a compassionate and progressive nation, we need a new renaissance in both the media and politics. If all Britain can rely upon for information is a combination of fake news and hate news, we can't survive.

To my mind, it was always a testament to my parents' essential decency that they never blamed outside migrants for their unemployment. They knew the true culprits were the rich who wanted to make profit regardless of the human suffering it caused.

My father may have placed no blame on others for our plight but my mother couldn't stop pointing the finger at my dad as the culprit in our downfall. It was my mum's way of justifying her continuing affair with the navvy, which had become an intense irrational tryst. My mother deluded herself into believing she could have a normal life with her lover and that no one would stop her. She enrolled my sister and me into a Catholic school because her lover was an Irishman. So, we converted to the faith of the one true church, despite the fact I don't ever recall going to Sunday services before our sudden baptism into religion.

However, while the priest of our parish was teaching me my catechism, my mother's affair with O'Sullivan began to cause outrage among the other tenants. After a while, our staying at the doss became untenable; eventually, we were evicted because of my mum's alleged impropriety to polite unemployed working-class society.

Their affair, however, didn't end with the termination of our lodgings but continued to smoulder in the ruins of my parents' doomed marriage. In a scene of high drama after we'd moved to a new doss, my mum screamed out to my dad, 'I'd rather kill myself than spend another hour in your company.' She didn't commit suicide. Instead, she fled in the night like a working-class Anna Karenina with her lover to St Albans as he had found work down there.

Many weeks later, she returned and appeared at the door of our room in the new doss holding in her hand a pineapple, bought in exotic London before her train departed north, as if she was Captain Cook returned from his travels in the South Seas. My father took her back without a word of reproach. However, after a short while, my mother confessed to him that she had abandoned us in Bradford because she was pregnant with her Irish navvy's child.

'Then why did you come back?' I heard my father ask her in our cramped quarters.

'He didn't want me with a baby,' was her response. And so there it was – my mum had thrown herself into the arms of another man in the expectation that he could save her but instead he did the opposite and doomed her.

In the autumn of that year, my half-brother Matthew was born and soon after we did a flit and ended up moving as close as possible to hell on this side of the earth. It was called St Andrew's Villas but, like in Dante's *Inferno*, there should have been a sign for all those who entered to abandon all hope.

It was in that dingy doss that my mother, still restless, still looking for escape from my father and our poverty, met up with another man named Bill Moxon. They had known each other in childhood and perhaps even desired each other as teens, and now in their thirties they became lovers. To protect

116

her relationship with Moxon and allow it to flourish rather than fall victim to the cruel gossip that had blighted her affair with the navvy, my mother instructed my sister Alberta and me to forever refer to our dad as Grandfather.

'Keep the eyes of the other bloody tenants off our backs,' said my mum to me, as she wanted strangers to think that she was married to Bill Moxon. 'Tell them that your dad died a long time ago if they ask where he be.' It was possible to convince others that my dad was my grandfather because the years of unemployment and poverty had aged him, making him bald, stooped and timid whereas my mother at the time was still radiantly beautiful.

As the room my mother took with Moxon was too small to house my sister, myself and my father comfortably, we were relocated to an unheated, unlit garret in the attic of the dosshouse where my father, sister and I slept together on one filthy mattress. My new brother, however, slept in a dresser drawer beside my mother in the room she now shared with Bill Moxon, the cowman.

My family was completely fractured by the lie my mother had concocted. Even though my sister and I kept to the story that our dad was our grandfather, it hurt and caused enormous damage to my emotional wellbeing. It made me feel that I had betrayed him as a son by denying his paternity in the company of others.

In the end, it sullied the love we held for our mother because we were never 100 per cent sure whether she did this for our survival or hers. But then again, even the strongest spirit is strained during a time of enormous crisis and upheaval, which is why over time I grew to accept that my mother was more sinned against than sinning.

As for Moxon, his introduction into our family didn't end our suffering. In fact, it brought an added dimension to it because he liked to drink and suffered from a violent temperament. Moreover, Moxon's infatuation with my mother never extended to her children because he was parsimonious with his cash, and we were just as hungry as before.

Our circumstances became so unsettled that, in the autumn of 1930, my mother had me indentured, at the age of seven, to an off licence that was situated down the road from our doss. Make no mistake, this was not a part-time job for a child, like a paper round or doing chores around the house; this was servitude and bondage to the owner of the shop. Child labour was rife in the 1930s because you could pay a child pennies to do a man's job. It's why I was put to work on a beer barrow that had metal wheels that came up to my chin. I pushed it through the mean streets of Bradford every weekday afternoon until well past sunset, as well as Saturdays. My job was to sell beer to the down-and-out of my community. It was hard work replete with dangers of being robbed or sexually abused by unsavoury characters.

When I began my first day of servitude, my mother said to me in anger and in guilt, 'It's a cocked-up world when a boy is sent to do a man's job.' Later on in life, she asked me to forgive her for what she did to me by making me work so hard when I was a young boy that it made me incapable of advancing in my school work. 'Wasn't you,' I said, 'it was the situation and the times that made you.'

By December 1930, the Great Depression had settled upon Britain with the virulence of a medieval plague that only targeted the poor, the vulnerable and the struggling middle class. As the cold weather closed in upon us, I traversed the streets of my neighbourhood hawking beer from my barrow and feeling an immense loneliness because I knew there was no adult who was going to rescue me from the hell of my waking world.

When Christmas morning came that year, I awoke like too many children across Britain with hunger in my belly and the realisation that there was no Father Christmas for the poor.

I remember crying in anger and desperation. My dad tried to calm my agitation as best he could by hugging me and saying, 'Go into my trouser pocket. It's not from Father Christmas and it's not much but it is from thy dad.'

I went over and rustled through his pockets and found a few bits of penny sweets that I ate for my breakfast.

Afterwards, I went down to the cramped room my mother shared with her boyfriend. She told me there'd be no Christmas lunch but, because we were Catholics, the church would provide us bairns with a bit of turkey and some comfort and joy down in a hall near the cathedral.

In a state of subdued despair, I attended mass and gave thanks like all of the other indigent children to the mercy of Jesus and his benevolent church, which was about to feed us.

Afterwards, we were led into a gymnasium where a Father Christmas with a tubercular cough gave me a pair of socks and an orange speckled with decay.

After I finished my Christmas meal, I walked home with my sister to our doss and tried to avoid looking into the windows of the houses that were along the way. I suppose I was afraid that I would see families unlike mine able to afford and celebrate the season.

At home, I found my father upstairs in the attic, chewing on a pipe starved of tobacco, reading a book in the grey light leaking into the room from a small window. He smiled at me and said, 'Happy Christmas, lad. Sorry there weren't much for thee and thy sister. Next year, hey son, next year . . .'

However, by the first week of 1931, my dad was forced to move out of our lives at the request of my mum's new boyfriend. One morning he was with us in the garret and by evening when I returned from work at the off licence, he was gone. He wasn't even allowed to say goodbye because, I guess, my mum believed that it was best for him to just leave. Five weeks shy of my eighth birthday I was told to forget him as if he had never existed or had died. So, he became like my dead sister Marion: a ghost that haunted both my waking and sleeping life. Now in the twilight of my life, I know why my dad left my sister and me in January 1931 without even a wave goodbye. It's because he realised he couldn't feed his wife or children; he left our dosshouse in the hope that without him we'd have a better chance to survive. I never saw my dad again and during my adolescence didn't know for sure if he was alive or dead; he just disappeared into the waste lands of Bradford that were ravaged by the sadism of unemployment and virulent poverty.

Thirteen years after he left, I was informed in a letter from my sister that our dad had died. It was 1943 and I was stationed with my RAF unit in the south of England. After reading the contents of that short letter I got drunk alone in a pub. I tried to mourn a man who I had been told to forget about as a boy and it hurt me so much to think that he'd been betrayed by everyone, including me. After the war, his two sisters tracked me down to a flat I shared with my wife in Halifax. They'd come to give me my inheritance. You see he'd died a pauper but had asked his sisters before he succumbed to pneumonia to sell the painting of their father and give the proceeds to my sister and myself. He had been dead many years by the time they had found me but they wanted me to have my share of his legacy, which amounted to ten shillings. Those coins when I held them felt as precious to me as a king's ransom.

These horrors of economics, of betrayed love, I relate to you are not unique to me – millions of my generation suffered the same or worse during the Great Depression. It is what mobilised us to fight and build a Britain we could be proud of and where our children could flourish after the Second World War. My only hope is that the similar pain that many people experience today will anger them as much as it did me and help forge a new nation from the ashes of grave injustice.

After my dad was made to vanish, the world around me began to feel more unstable, dark and fearful. I was orphaned from my father's gentleness. His absence greatly affected my emotional development because I was forced to become a man while still in short pants. As I grew so too did my sense of alienation from society, my country and the world. I felt I belonged to no family, community or nation because I couldn't understand how it was possible that I and my kind suffered more grievously than others in Britain because of the terrible effect the Great Depression had on the working class.

Rampant inequality was within sight because Bradford was a tale of two cities, one destitute and one that still thrived. Only a short walk from the garret I called home on St Andrew's Villas was the high street, which showed me how the other half lived. When I was on it, I felt like an animal that had stumbled out of a dark forest and now found itself in the midst of hostile creatures.

The high street was an unnatural environment for me because, when I walked down it on the days that I played truant from school, I was invisible to everyone else on the street. The other pedestrians couldn't see me because all they noticed was my exterior made rough from doss-house living. I was viewed by people of middle-class means, and those that were even better off than them, in the way one would observe a cat that happened to scamper out from an alley way or a pigeon cooing on a lamp post. I was like chewing gum stuck to the pavement. When well-dressed visitors to the high street took note of me, they skirted around me like I was an obstacle to avoid rather than a human being.

The opulence of inanimate luxury goods that decorated shop windows like pearls on a dowager sneered at my impecuniosity. I was intrigued and heart-broken by what I saw and knew I could never possess. All the things my family and my neighbours weren't able to afford arrogantly leered out at me – patent leather shoes, winter coats, scarves, trousers, suits and dresses. One time, as I salivated at these beautiful objects that kept one both warm and comfortable, shame rushed over me like effluence from a ruptured septic tank because I caught my reflection staring back at me from the window pane. The image I saw glaring at me was a filthy boy who wore a dusty cap and thick corduroy charity trousers that were held up by frayed suspenders. It shattered me to see myself as others saw me. I turned away from the display window in disgust. And, near tears, I began to walk forlornly home in boots whose soles were patched with newspaper and cardboard to keep the wet out.

It was then that emotionally I understood that the Britain I lived in was against me and my kind. It was simple: since my parents could not afford to buy themselves or me the goods for sale on the high street, I wasn't important enough to warrant compassion or humanity.

In some ways, the manner in which the shop-owners and their customers saw me as nothing more than working-class detritus matches how many of us view today's recipients of benefits, spurred on by the propaganda of the right-wing media and its lurid tales of welfare cheats and their addictions to both legal and illegal substances.

At every turn, good people in Britain are given an opportunity to excuse or reinforce their prejudices against the marginalised because most of the media is feeding into a narrative that says that poverty is a character defect rather than a failure of society to adequately protect its less fortunate. The Conservatives and UKIP's entire ideology is based upon wedge politics. The migration of war-weary individuals from Syria, Sudan, Afghanistan or a dozen other countries that are plagued by war or civil unrest fails to elicit sympathy in us because our politicians would prefer to deflect the blame on to the victims rather than our arms industry or our foreign policy. Both now and in the 1930s, refugees are dehumanised by language. It's cheaper in the short term to paint victims of war as criminals, rapists and fifth columnist Islamic fundamentalists rather than seek a solution to the conflicts from which these refugees have fled or to help them resettle.

I understood very early on in my life that I would always be on the outside of society looking in unless there was radical change to the way Britain treated all of its citizens.

You see, those window displays on that long-ago high street reminded the unemployed, the destitute, the vulnerable and me that, while there might have been 6 million men out of work, there was still a sizable minority who were immune to the plague of economic depression.

The worst realisation for me when I was young was that by and large many people just didn't care how we lived and how we suffered as long as they didn't have to see it.

While Yorkshire, Lancashire, Scotland, Wales, Cornwall and Northern Ireland starved, the bright young things in London danced until dawn and found their blithe spirits reflected in the plays of Noël Coward or the prose of Evelyn Waugh.

Today, I feel the same disconcertion I experienced when I was young if I visit a high street. When I am on Oxford Street, the shop windows today display a similar cornucopia. Yet, it all hangs out of reach of so many like a branch that dangles fruit high up on a tree, and I see the homeless begging for change outside the shops.

The feelings of alienation I had as a youth can be no different than what many of our young today experience, when they are made to feel inadequate because of their parents' lack of fiscal independence.

Yet in every region of our land, kids are doing without, in record numbers, because society has turned its back on compassion. Somehow politicians like Theresa May hope that if they ignore the issues causing these disparities in wealth and living standards long enough, they will disappear or we will all become as indifferent as the average Tory voter. It smacks of something more than hypocrisy when Theresa May addressed the Lord Mayor's banquet in November 2016 to warn us that inequality could breed a Donald Trump in Britain. But in 2017 she courts him like a suitor desperate for marriage. Moreover, it's rank cynicism because Theresa May is an insider, if not by birth by career and marriage to an executive City banker. Her wealth is as extreme as her beliefs and may well foster her refusal to tackle corporate tax avoidance.

Theresa May's entire political life has been spent upholding the rights of the elite at the expense of everyone else. As Home Secretary, she approved and championed vans that travelled to immigrant communities and announced through loud speakers and posters pasted onto the vehicle that it was the duty of all residents to inform the government of the whereabouts of illegal immigrants. We cannot believe politicians like May when they try to convince us they are making a serious commitment to ending the housing crisis when this Tory government is responsible for the least social housing built in a year since 1993.

When a Tory government or a right-wing government abroad is in power, the problem of inequality is never fixed. Instead, it is left untreated and it festers just like a poisoned wound. The world right now is oozing from those sores of inequality, which is why Eastern Europe is walking itself back to the age of fascism in the 1930s. Poland, Hungary and Bulgaria are all firmly fixed in the orbit of extreme right-wing politics while Ukraine is run by a billionaire kleptocrat who encourages fanaticism. The Czech Republic is run by an anti-migrant populist who talks of Islam as if it were an army of Saladin standing ready to invade Bohemia. Even the Baltic states are in peril because fear of Russian expansionism has them dangerously listing towards authoritarianism.

The longer Russia remains in the grasp of Vladimir Putin, the longer its own people will suffer the economic consequences of his dictatorship more than anyone else, but if we don't remedy inequality and the refugee crises, Putin's Russia will be the external threat that pushes Western democracies over the edge, especially now America has Donald Trump for president. Our entire world teeters perilously between oligarchy and dysfunctional democracy, which has been made worse by the rise of leaders like Trump, Putin and Xi Jinping in China.

Here in Britain, the EU referendum tore open the scab of globalisation. Decades of deindustrialisation in what were once Britain's manufacturing heartlands as well as an exponential transfer of wealth to the 1 per cent was just too much for many people in this country. Brexit proved that our nation has been profoundly affected by globalisation, which gave great wealth to the top tier of society and economic insecurities to the rest. Brexit has shown Britain to be like a cornered animal, frightened, irrational and likely to bite what feeds it just as much as what punishes it.

Inequality is the root of all revolutions from France in 1789 to Russia in 1917 and Germany in 1932. It's why no one should be surprised at the rise of Donald Trump. The reality TV show maven who made his fortune not from hard work but from the inheritance of his father's extreme wealth was able to tap into the anger of those abandoned by free-trade deals like NAFTA. Former assembly-line workers from America's rust belt, evangelicals outraged by being led by a liberal black president and business trying to return to the glory days of the robber barons each sought affirmation in Donald Trump's promise to 'Make America Great Again'. Trump's pledge and his political persona were forged in a cauldron of reality TV where reason is replaced by raw vituperative emotion. Sixty million people voted for him and did so neither with their heads nor their hearts, but instead used their spleen to secure him the presidency. Watching him be elected president was as chilling to me as my memories of the rise of Hitler. The politics of hate espoused by the Nazis and Donald Trump's bigoted rhetoric against minorities were produced in a similar primordial sea of economic duress. Unemployment may be only 4.5 per cent in America but when working full-time doesn't guarantee that you will have enough to put a roof over your head or feed your children, animosity will begin to boil over. Moreover, Obama may have fashioned himself as the president of hope and change but when corporate profits increased by 166 per cent and wages by only 3.4 per cent during his time in government, his message made many of his citizens more cynical about politics.

I understand the anger that drove people towards the cliff of Brexit or into the poisonous arms of Donald Trump because poverty shrank my possibilities just like a prison cell reduces a person's mobility and stunts their dreams. During the early 1930s, I knew I was trapped by my family's lack of financial resources. I had no dreams about growing up and having a good job. No politician had to tell me I had no future. I knew from the day I started pushing a beer barrow at the age of seven that my education, my childhood and my human dignity were being sacrificed because my family needed to eat and the state was unwilling to supply us with what we needed to survive.

Each time my mother watered down our porridge or made me go to a neighbour's room to beg for bread, I knew that life is more than tough, it is unfair – similarly, a person today knows this when their gas or electric is cut off because of non-payment. Knowing that my poverty constrained not only my present but my future made me disgruntled by my circumstances even when very young. After my dad left, I began to grow outraged by our poverty and by what it forced each one of my family to do to get by. I was livid, ashamed and even disgusted at the way my mum had to ingratiate herself with her boyfriend, a man prone to violence when touched by drink. It angered me that my sister Alberta not only worked like me but knew that, simply because she was female, that her chances of getting out of poverty were slim to none. At the age of thirteen, she said to me, 'When you grow up, Harry, you'll be able to fly out and off of this shit pile like a little bird. But me, I am not going anywhere because I am a girl and my wings are already broken.'

Some of my contemporaries took consolation in the words of our priest at Sunday mass but I couldn't. Sure, our parish priest talked a good game in a church filled to the rafters with a congregation that had been made devout by their hunger and unemployment. They came to church to find answers on how to play the miserable set of cards life had dealt them. But the church offered no earthly solutions to poverty. Our priest's only reply was that if we had been good then paradise awaited us in the hereafter, while hell's damnation was assured for those who weren't. I didn't buy his words because I preferred, no matter how painful to accept, my mother's homilies on what paradise meant for folks like us: 'Both the politicians and priests keep us under their thumb by making promises they know we can never collect from them. Lad, there's nowt behind those pearly gates you can't find out back in the midden – it's all shite.'

No, poverty made me feel trapped as there seemed to be no means to escape it. Poverty cornered me and put me against the wall. Poverty made me feel like I was no more than a caged animal waiting to be slaughtered. It made me feel like the pig my mum's boyfriend and I had cornered before we killed it at the farm where he tended to the livestock. We'd nicked the pig because times were tough and when my mum's man saw an opportunity, legitimate or otherwise, to get a leg up on those who held him down, he took it without thinking twice.

At the time of the killing, I was ten and in equal measure

130

Bill frightened me, angered me and beguiled me. So, when he ordered me to come with him to slaughter a pig, I followed him with the same blindness that I followed my sergeant major at induction in 1941.

When he made me pen a pig into a corner of a cement stall, I did it even though it sickened me. 'Hold piggy's head while I go bash his brains in with a hammer,' he said to me in a guttural accent that was empty of hard syllables because all his teeth had been pulled out a long time ago.

The pig's eyes were filled with both fear and anger. I held on to his contorting skull while shit fell out of his backside. It took several blows to kill the animal and the hammer came down with the same brutality as if it were a domestic murder. Bits of brain were over the front of my coat and my boots were covered in the dead animal's shit while my stomach churned with revulsion at what I had done.

After my mum's boyfriend had slaughtered the pig, he noticed that the animal's death had upset me and he tried to comfort me by saying, 'It was him or us, lad, him or us. Just think of the crackling that's for your tea tonight.'

There is no dignity in being poor because it leaves you at the mercy of the mighty and the ordinary. Wondering where your next meal is going to come from doesn't build character; it only creates shame, humiliation, self-loathing and resentment. I know that for the millions who live under the poverty line in twenty-first-century Britain, my feelings of inadequacy in the 1930s are not alien concepts. My salvation was to become politicised and it must become the salvation of today's marginalised if they are to ever hope to fight back the tide of conservatism that is robbing people of their dignity. It's why those on the left must begin to act again like they did in the 1930s, 1940s and 1950s as equals in the struggle to free the working class of not only their poverty but their ignorance of politics. They must begin to proselytise like they once did across working-class neighbourhoods, to the poor, to the vulnerable and to new immigrants. Today, all of us who are interested in making a more equal country have to start telling our friends, neighbours and strangers that the only hope of good schools for our kids or grandkids is not through academies or grammars but by the government investing real money into our communities.

Those on the left must counter the propaganda being churned out by the right wing that benefits recipients are cheats and that the working class has been betrayed by our membership of the EU or by the free movement of labour. The enemies of wage earners aren't immigrants or those in receipt of benefits; their mortal foes are the corporations that suppress wages and hide profits offshore by legal means. People have to use their time in shop queues, church meeting halls, mosques, synagogues, temples, lunch rooms and on the train ride home to talk about the real abuses working people face each day because of Tory-induced austerity, not to chat about the match of the day. We must wake up to the realisation that democracy only works if we are educated enough to understand the dilemmas we face as a nation and individuals.

For me, the only way I was able to escape that feeling of being trapped in an existence that offered no escape was through the power of books I found to read at our local library.

It enrages me that the simple right to civilisation that a local library provides to its neighbourhoods is being denied to so many in Britain today. Across this nation our libraries are being shuttered at an alarming rate because of an ideologically driven austerity. One in eight council-run libraries has been closed due to budget cutbacks. Moreover, for those still in operation their fiscal allotment has been clawed back by a fifth since 2010. Closing libraries isn't about being financially prudent, it's about closing the minds of millions of citizens to the benefits of literature, history and philosophy, and shuttering their imaginations to the beauty and brilliance of ideas.

When my dad let me have a penny to get a library membership, it was one of the greatest gifts he ever gave to me. His investment has provided me with an incalculable profit to both my mind and spirit for the last eighty-seven years. If I had not had access to a library during the Great Depression I don't think I would have survived the trauma of that time. At the very least, without the books I read from libraries, I would not have been literate because our nomadic lifestyle had seriously upset my primary years of education. To this day, it still amazes me that despite the squalor of the era I grew up in, where good healthcare, education and housing were entirely dependent upon your income, libraries were abundant, cheap to join and welcoming to the working class.

I learned much from the words of my uncles who still toiled in the coal pits of Barnsley. They taught me that only collective action, trade unionism or education could change our country's economic landscape. My education came not from my schooling, which ended at fourteen as was the custom of the time for the working class, but from the streets, my parents and the people I interacted with as a boy and young man. But it was literature that taught me about myself and about the profundities of the human heart.

At the libraries I frequented as a boy, I was able to borrow books of fairy stories and Aesop's fables. The first books I borrowed were used by my father and then my elder sister Alberta to improve my letters, diction and comprehension. Over time, the library became for me a place of refuge because the books I read let me sail to a hundred different countries, learn about foreign cultures or discover the beauty of poetry.

In my teenage years, I read Robert Tressell's *The Ragged-trousered Philanthropists*. It taught me that the British working class had never been given a fair deal and that it had been under a yoke of oppression for centuries. The works of Charles Dickens, Victor Hugo and Émile Zola let me know that injustice to the poor was universal, immoral and could be overcome through the power of art, literature and politics. I soon had enough knowledge to make the argument that the poverty of my class was not caused because we were feckless, morally inferior or intellectually lacking but because the system, like today, favoured the ruling class by not taxing property or wealth sufficiently, valued greed over equality, and kept working people enslaved to employers who were not obliged by law to pay a fair wage or provide safe working conditions.

My love of books eased my loneliness and gave me a sense of belonging to something greater. When I first read the Lake Poets I thought they were speaking to me directly. Each time I read a new book, I felt like Howard Carter when he opened up the tomb of Tut and was asked by a companion standing behind him what he saw and replied, 'I see wonderful things.'

At thirteen I rode a rickety old bike from Halifax to York to visit the Minster for the first time. It was a great adventure for a lad like me, whose imagination had been set free by Robert Louis Stevenson, to ride to that city that had been around since the days of the Roman conquest. But when I saw that great cathedral my first impressions weren't about religious adoration. No, my faith had been lost through the numerous canings and humiliations I'd received from the priests and nuns who'd tried to teach me that Jesus' love should draw blood and blind obedience. My epiphany came not from a supernatural being but from awe at the Minster's architectural beauty. I felt energised and ennobled by the majesty of this building. I recognised it took the hands of a thousand anonymous artisans to build a cathedral that was the envy of the medieval world, just like it took tens of thousands of men like my father in the pits to establish a modern industrialised nation.

Standing in front of the minster and recognising its aesthetic magnificence made me realise that despite the poverty of my life, the hunger of my birth, the loss of my dad and the growing estrangement of my mother, I could still recognise and enjoy beauty. It meant I was human. An indifferent society had categorised me as something that was expendable, unworthy of healthcare, unworthy of housing, unworthy of an education, unworthy of a job that paid a decent salary, but I was worth more than that. I was worth more than the casual indifference I received on the high streets of Yorkshire towns from people who had the privilege of both a good education and good work. I knew from my emotional reaction at seeing this cathedral that I would be able to liberate myself from my grim surroundings. Words, books, history, art and the politics of socialism would build me a bridge to a better land.

My feelings proved to me that I was different, unique and had worth regardless of whether society believed that I warranted consideration. It taught me that I mattered and that I'd never let anyone or any political system try to steal my dignity from me again.

Chapter Eight:
Forsaken by an Economy for the Rich

In 2016, St Andrew's Villas still look desolate and forsaken. What was once our doss still stands but it is now a mosque, which gives my soul much comfort. But its facade still holds the same melancholic dilapidation it exuded in the 1930s. Staring at it, I can hear the tormented cries of those who once inhabited rooms underneath its roof – abandoned pensioners, soldiers and families all thrown overboard by a society more interested in catering to the whims of its elite class. This place was a ground zero, if you will, for my family because it was on this street we took the full blast from the Great Depression. My family lost so much of themselves here; hope, trust, love. Almost everything that made us human was abandoned here.

There are fewer buildings on the street but what stands looks forlorn, neglected and ashamed. It hurts to see that poverty hasn't disappeared from this neighbourhood. Penury still clings to St Andrew's Villas.

Unless Britain returns to a more progressive politics, so many streets, towns and regions will remain shrouded in the sadness of people's lives truncated by economic events beyond their control. No good came from Britain re-electing David Cameron's Tories into government in 2015. Their small working majority delivered not only more austerity and financial deregulation but also the Act that paved the way for the EU referendum and now Brexit. Surely, the last six years should have instructed everyone that Tories don't make social policies to assist those without advantages.

I am not going to pretend it doesn't pain me to return to this street and see my old haunt. Coming back here is always difficult because it is just another unmarked graveyard for my childhood. The omnipresence of hopelessness gives me a lump in my throat and makes me want to shout out into the damp atmosphere, 'Try as you might austerity, you didn't break me.' But I know that isn't true because the Great Depression did bust me up spiritually, emotionally and mentally. Were it not for the creation of a more progressive society after the war, and my luck in finding the love of my life in 1945, I would never have survived to be almost a hundred years old. No, without those two things I would have perished from the damage done to my spirit as a lad. I would have been destroyed by the rage fuelled by drink and joblessness that I saw overcome some of my younger relatives.

I worry what will happen to young people today who are being assailed by both austerity and the consequences of Brexit because for them there is little hope for a brighter tomorrow. I think there is a gathering storm of fury building up in our younger members of society and, if it is unleashed, it will not be pretty. Unless we are careful, the decline in truthful reporting and sincere politicians will help fuel the risk of mob rule and mob violence. We are sitting on a powder keg of resentment caused by austerity, which is being deflected by the Tories and their press to migrants, minorities and the poor. That's why, as long as I am able, I will not stop speaking at venues across this country to tell our young that they are this country's future and that they must follow the path my generation trod after the Second World War. If they ever hope to find economic and social fulfilment, they must look to revolutionise the economy, like we did in 1945. It will not be easy, it will not be quick but it must be done.

What always most affects me when I return to St Andrew's Villas is seeing the garret window that gave light to the attic where I slept with my sister and father on a flock mattress. Beneath the thin pane of glass, I kipped there frozen in winter, dank in spring, humid in summer, damp in autumn. In the morning, the anaemic rays of the sun used to fall limply against the glass and wake me from unquiet dreams. In rain storms, the window leaked and water rolled down the side of the ceiling, and I thought it was like being in the hold of a ship slowly taking on water.

Under thick clouds in the spring of 2016, with the air pregnant with rain and my collar turned upwards, I looked at that garret window and wept to myself. Seeing it, I heard my dad's kind voice trying to wash away my melancholy. 'It's all right, lad, we've got each other and that is no small matter.' But in the end we didn't even have each other because everything was dissolved in the hard acid bath of our poverty.

Seeing that lonely window, I also recalled the wild mouse I'd tried to tame to keep my sister and me company. But that mouse wasn't spared either because once my mum found it she crushed it under her shoe. 'We can't afford to be giving food to vermin.'

Nothing was spared then – all decency, kindness and even love was thrown overboard to keep ourselves afloat. As an adult I am glad the welfare state and a public NHS protected me from ever having to make the tough decisions my parents had to make for their children. But today, other parents all across this country are being forced to make hard choices about their lives and their children's lives because right-wing politicians don't see the harm that their policy of austerity has brought to our many neighbourhoods.

In fact, they even profit from the misery of others. Iain Duncan Smith, architect of benefits sanctions, now demands £500 for an hour's talk to service clubs, while George Osborne has earned hundreds of thousands of pounds for speaking to American bank executives and boasting of his failed and shameful economic experiment.

What happened to all those who lived here in St Andrew's Villas when I was a lad? Did they survive not only the Great Depression but also the Second World War? Were they able to see the building of the welfare state? Were they and their kids provided a life that had happiness, purpose and dignity? Or did they all perish before then? A childhood mate of mine named Trevor didn't make it past twenty-one. When I was a boy, I loved him like a brother – it was easy to because his family showed me a kindness that I rarely encountered in my youth. His father had a heart as wide as the sea and sometimes he invited me to join them for their tea, and his wife always made sure I could bring something back for my sister. On other occasions, Trevor's dad paid for my ticket to a Saturday movie matinee at the Odeon cinema.

When we left St Andrew's Villas I lost track of him. Many years later I ran into his sister at a butcher's shop. In between asking the man behind the counter for a bit of rationed bacon and him wrapping it in paper, his sister told me, 'Trevor died fighting Rommel in the desert.'

My youth was grim but it would have been brutally cruel were it not for the fact that the misery of those days was shared by many other kids who befriended me in this former slum.

It's why when darkness came and my work for the off licence was done, I never returned straight away to the savagery of my dosshouse. Instead, I'd take to the narrow, dark streets of my warren because, in the darkness, I felt that I could escape despair by playing rough games with fellow chums.

Under evening's black canvas just before Bonfire Night, the children of this neighbourhood set their misery aside in the pursuit of wild games that could be as violent as skirmishes in a guerrilla war. In late and early November days, we invaded derelict buildings that had been shuttered by the economic catastrophe. In the gloaming, we'd scavenged for wood for the fires we'd light to remember the fifth of November. But also we foraged for old factory pulley ropes that were greased with oil and took them outside. On those narrow, cobbled streets, we used Captain Webb matches to light their ends until they smouldered and glowed bright red like the tip of a cigarette in the dark night air. We'd sing childish rhymes about monkeys shitting limes. Then, intoxicated by the ecstasy of play, we'd spin the hemp tapers around in the air until the frayed bits sparked against the blackness. Emboldened like Prometheus bringing fire to mankind, we'd run through the streets hollering our delight. In those moments of play, we forgot hunger, loneliness and sadness. But the joy was as brief as a warm summer's day in Bradford because misery in our neighbourhood was always just around the corner.

At times, as we traipsed across our patch in the dead of night, our merriment was stopped in its tracks by inhuman noises. The sounds tumbling out from nearby open windows may have been inhuman, but they weren't ever inanimate. No, they were cries of pain and of torment. Sometimes they came from women being beaten senseless by their husbands or, in other instances, children suffering the wrath of their fathers, who in unemployed angst had taken to both drink and blind fury. Other times, the cries that came from open windows sounded like howls from a circle of hell that even my parish priest would have been reluctant to admit existed. But they were not the growls of the damned, just the screams from people who were too poor to pay for morphine to ease their pain from cancer and make their passage to the next world gentle rather than grotesque.

Any time I think of the billion-pound shortfall the NHS faces because of Tory cutbacks to our public healthcare system, I hear those cries of unendurable pain that leaped out from windows in my boyhood neighbourhood. All that pain and anguish came because people didn't have the money to pay for either medical services or pharmaceutical drugs. It is disturbing that both the Conservative Party and UKIP are lukewarm to a public NHS. In fact, Paul Nuttall, the leader of UKIP, was a strong proponent of privatisation before he joined his political party. UKIP seems to be a platform that is indifferent to facts and subservient to fascism. They don't see the NHS as important and that is perhaps because they are rich enough to afford private healthcare. If the public doesn't demand that its politicians consider public healthcare sacrosanct, it will disappear.

To forget my memories, or to forget the memories of your own parents and grandparents, is to forget that everyone but the very well off is vulnerable in a society that only values money. My generation, for all its many faults, believed in the sanctity of public ownership of our state assets, which is why we nationalised key industries after the war. We wanted them to work for us, not just private shareholders.

For me, playing nocturnal games in alleyways littered with dismal dosshouses was only ever a brief respite from the tragedies occurring within my family. I hated living in that doss and what I was forced to do and see. It was worse for me once my dad had gone because there was no one to absorb my mum's disappointments and anxieties. Ever since we had left Barnsley, my mother's moods had become erratic and her reason unstable from the stress of our living conditions. She was also beginning to be overwhelmed by the guilt she felt for putting my father out into the streets, which manifested itself by her taking to drink and sarcasm. Her family was little support to her during those days because they viewed her as a fallen woman for taking up with another man. On the occasions I did visit my grandparents in the 1930s, my mum's name was rarely mentioned and my younger brother Matt was forbidden to join my sister and me owing to the fact that he was illegitimate. Her ostracism did not end until both my grandparents had died, and then her siblings, who were just as irascible as her, reconciled in their shared memories of hard-fought lives.

It didn't help my mum's mental health that her boyfriend Bill drank and when angered by her would threaten to leave us. 'I'll be gone by morning and then you'll be right buggered and in the poor house by week's end.' My sister and I hoped he'd get on his bike but my mother was terrified of that eventuality.

In a misguided belief that she was saving us by living with Bill, my mum lost her ability to be a good parent. She was more afraid of displeasing our bread winner than of harming us. My mum began to treat my sister and me as lodgers whose only value was measured by the money we accumulated through our working activities. She even began to search the garret where my sister and I slept when we were out working or at school to see if we'd hidden any money from our wages. Once she found a piggy bank I'd concealed under a loose floorboard and smashed it open to loot its contents. When I confronted her and accused her of stealing from me, my mum retorted, 'Without me and my cunning, you'd already be dead in the street. Hide any brass from me and you'll get more than a broken piggy bank the next time.'

The Great Depression had brutalised my mother's spirit just as much as war corrupts the morality of those who are sent to fight in them. My mum turned from a person who was generally good and tried to lead a moral life into an embittered individual who was distrustful of everyone's motives. She medicated her anxiety by drinking more than she should. It was as if in consuming cheap gin she could forget what had happened to us and what awaited us in this maelstrom of poverty.

My mum was trying to do her best but, like a ship whose masts have broken in a hurricane, she was about to capsize.

The stress of trying to keep her three children and herself in her boyfriend Bill's good books was wearing her down. Still, she had little choice but to stick it out with him.

She realised that without him all she could hope for was poor relief, which virtually guaranteed that my sister and I would be sent to a workhouse for the rest of our youth. 'It's him or the poor house' was a constant threat that my mum dangled in front of my nose if I questioned the logic of living under the mean shadow of her man Bill. To her there was no other solution but remaining with Bill no matter how much he terrorised us or her.

When the social safety network was constructed between 1945 and 1979, it was built to prevent children like my sister and me from being harmed by the vagaries of an unjust economic system. The welfare state ensured that parents who were at risk of mental illness because of financial issues could be helped before their conditions became tragic for not only themselves but the children they cared for. That's why affordable housing and adequate benefits, along with provisions for social workers to assist at-risk individuals, were the cornerstone of the modern progressive state.

Today, however, after seven years of Tory government cuts to both mental health services in the NHS and to the number of social workers in any given community, at-risk people are grievously suffering. They hurt just like my mum did over eighty years ago when she was marooned with her three kids in a dosshouse in an unfriendly part of Bradford.

Today, parents at risk of mental health issues created by the stress of living under a perpetual regime of economic and social austerity know they are on very thin ice, thanks to the endless cuts to benefits for those in work or out.

When it comes to mental health treatment in Britain, there should be no waiting times but the wait for help for psychiatric problems is now almost endless thanks to the Tory belief that if you can't afford it, you don't need it.

It can now take upwards of six months from a GP's referral before a patient gets their first assessment from a psychiatrist. That is too long and lives have been lost because of it. Karl Turner, the Labour MP for Hull, discovered this in the most tragic way when his nephew, a young articling law student, took his own life after being put on a six-month wait list to see a psychiatrist to address a deterioration in his mental health.

As for social workers, their case loads are so large these days that a recent report commissioned by HCPC found that time spent with clients was becoming desperately and dangerously limited. Moreover, the less time a social worker has with a client the more likely mental health issues, from depression to psychosis or addiction, will be overlooked. Social workers, because of austerity, now have to take the same attitude as front-line medics in the Second World War, which means they only treat those who can be saved with limited intervention. This is not the way a modern society should be run. It is not only cruel but contemptuous of human life for a government to dictate who lives and who dies. And you know damn well that the neighbours of Theresa May will always get the best cut from life because, like her, they are the 1 per cent.

For all those who get lost in the shuffle or are denied timely treatment, the fault isn't bureaucracy at the NHS; the fault is at the hands of David Cameron and now his successor Theresa May, who have prioritised the rapid creep of privatisation over good healthcare in England.

Looking back, there is no question that my mum needed emotional support and, if possible, counselling. But in her day, the only help available to working-class people who suffered from mental health issues was going to come from family or friends. But, in so many ways, living in our slum was like living in a war zone, so few people had the time to show consideration to someone else. It wasn't that people didn't want to help; it was that they were too over-whelmed with trying to survive themselves to give much assistance.

Everybody in our doss or in the dosses across the street, down the road or the next street over had an equally horrific life. Everyone was hungry, everyone was scrambling for work, everyone was desperate to survive and this tragedy was happening all across Britain.

Everybody was scared of what was to become of them and each one of us was without remedy for our problems. Once, in an attempt to borrow a slice of bread from another doss-house inmate, I stumbled into a room where a man's wife showed the onset of Parkinson's disease – her limbs shuddered and jerked as if they were controlled by an evil puppeteer.

Soldiers from the Great War littered our neighbourhood like spent pop bottles on the common. They were everywhere and each of them seemed to be suffering from a peace that delivered them nothing but hunger. On the streets, I stumbled into former Tommies talking to themselves in tortured rhyme, or in states of drunkenness, calling for dead comrades whose corpses had long been mouldering in graves near the now calm battlefields of France. Some of those staying in our doss had been gassed so badly they coughed incessantly through the days and the nights of their bitter, breathless existence. The slums across Britain were like a triage ward with no doctors or nurses; only patients screaming for relief, knowing none was ever going to be found.

Still, people understood that it shouldn't have to be this way. People knew then that compassion must also be an instrument of the state, just as much as a national army was there to protect Britain from foreign threats. But we had to wait until we were almost annihilated by austerity and then the Second World War before we were able to demand a welfare state that flowed with the milk of human kindness through practical and not extravagant socialism.

But for my mother the wait was too long. So, without help or just a gentle hand to assuage her anxiety, my mum's mental frame work began to fall apart. Her panic attacks became more pronounced and she was treated as a hysteric by Bill because she believed she was going to die. On occasions, my mother also became very cruel to both friend and foe alike if she was under extreme mental stress.

Once, after coming home from a movie matinee, I came upon her in the common room of our doss. Overjoyed and overwhelmed by watching comedic movie shorts starring Buster Keaton and Harold Lloyd, I rushed to tell her of my adventure at the Odeon. Somehow, my childish enthusiasm irritated her. At that moment, she was breastfeeding my younger brother Matthew. In a pique, she pulled her breast from my brother's hungry mouth and pumped her milk into my face. The milk ran down me and on to my filthy shirt. Tears welled up in my eyes that were equal parts shame and hatred for my mum who had humiliated me in front of strangers in a deranged temper. My mum rubbed her venom further into my heart by sarcastically bellowing out, 'Don't be crying now because I did you a good turn considering you are always moaning how hungry you are.'

She had stung me hard and I ran up to my garret room sobbing.

However, my rage for my mother soon passed because I began to realise that she was being abused by her man Bill. At first, their arguments were loud rumblings that had the ferocity of a thunder storm. But, after a while, Bill's temper took a turn for the worse and that was because his job at the pig farm was under threat. He began punctuating his differences of opinion with my mum over money or drink with a fist. The first time I saw him strike her, she was preparing tea. My mother had upset Bill by pressing him for the week's housekeeping money. It wasn't a lethal blow – more like the way some people with a hard temperament discipline a dog by using the back of their hand.

It was a turning point in their relationship because my mum was strong and, throughout her life, she had bowed to no one and nothing. However, because leaving Bill assured that we would either starve or be sent to a workhouse, she submitted to Bill's brutality. The type of physical and later on sexual assaults my mum underwent happen to many women today. This is why it is incumbent upon a civilised nation to provide safety for those under threat from their partners. But here again, because of austerity, there are fewer places for women to take shelter and to be safe from their abusers. Aid, a domestic violence charity, estimated in 2016 that, due to welfare reform, two-thirds of refuges for women in England and Wales faced closure. If we can afford to do tax deals with Google, Britain can certainly afford to adequately fund women's shelters and stop torture at the hands of their partners.

After that first slap, Bill kept hitting my mother for another two years without much of a schedule to his wrath. Some things wouldn't bother him and he brushed them aside like hair that had fallen into his eyes. When I lost half a crown with which I was supposed to pay the butcher and my mum took the blame for losing it, he said nothing, even though money was always tight. Other matters, like a mark on his only good shirt that he wore down at the pub, and my mum would have to keep away from him because he was rabid dog for days.

It wasn't until 1934, when Bill got a job at a rendering plant in Sowerby Bridge and we moved to new digs, that his physical attacks on my mother became as routine as the stops on a bus route.

When we left Bradford for Sowerby Bridge without our dad, I knew that whatever happened to us in the future, one thing was for certain: we were a family that was held together more by shame and anger than love. I also realised as the bus departed the city limits that it was unlikely I'd ever see my father in this lifetime. And I recalled with sadness what he had told me when we first arrived in Bradford: 'There is a chance for us in this big city to do all right as long as we stay strong and always act as a family.' When we left Bradford I was only eleven, but all I had done and seen made me feel like I was a very old man.

Chapter Nine:
2008 – World on the Brink of Ruin

My life is nearly all gone. Time has turned it to ash like newspaper print that flies up the chimney flue after it has been lit to start the fire on a winter's eve.

For most of my days, I believed that my experiences as a young man before the welfare state weren't that unique. Almost everyone I knew had similar stories of loss and hardship. If they hadn't been affected by the Great Depression they found their sorrow during the war. I looked at the road ahead of me instead of behind because it was just too painful to linger in the past.

However, after the financial crash that began with the banking crisis in 2007, I couldn't ignore the events that happened to me during the Great Depression. I couldn't look away because the world's banks hadn't been this near total ruin since 1929. My history and the history of my generation seemed more relevant than ever. I was over-whelmed by ancient memories of soup kitchens, midnight flits, living on the rough side of society. In my imagin-ation, I kept on seeing and tasting the images of squalor I'd kept hidden away from myself and others for most of my life. The aroma of hopelessness hung over my child-hood and everyone in working-class Britain like a putrid fog that didn't begin to lift until the war blew it all away in 1939.

It all came back to me with a vibrancy that was both sad and profound while I sat alone in a Portuguese *pastelaria* and washed down a custard tart with a strong espresso cof-fee. I had been a widower since 1999 and in 2010 found myself living in Albufeira after the death of my middle son Peter the year earlier had caused me to exile myself and my grief to Portugal's Algarve district. His death had hit me hard. He had died from IPF – idiopathic pulmonary fibro-sis, a fatal and incurable lung disease – at the age of fifty, having battled schizophrenia for the past twenty-five years of his life. The grief over his death was as painful as torture to me. It's why I left all that was familiar; I wanted to escape the burdens of my existence and find my own death on the warm coastline of Portugal. I thought I was ready to die but death, however, didn't come for me, no matter how much I longed for it to release me from my sorrow, my guilt and my anger over losing a child.

I was being water-boarded by grief over his death and all the sorrows from my youth also came back to harass me like a merciless gang of thugs. Yet in between the agony of remembering my son and acknowledging that all human life ends in defeat, I was becoming aware that our modern world was being beaten out of shape by the same economic hammer that had been used to bash apart my childhood. Austerity was back and this time it was coming for my grandchildren's generation.

Britain and America may have bailed out the banks but the financial stability of individuals was all gone, eaten away by both personal debt and precarious work. It felt like it was 1929 except this time there was social media to document the collapse of the economy. But in the twenty-first century there was no FDR on the horizon to initiate a New Deal for the people. At first, I thought Obama might have been like Roosevelt and saved the ordinary people through honest work projects and economic reform. Instead, Obama protected the wealth of the richest citizens through quantitative easing as well as by failing to prosecute any of the banking executives who had bust the world's economy out of personal greed and sheer incompetence.

It meant that last orders were about to be called on the social welfare state and democracy because the 1 per cent weren't about to share their untaxed wealth to get us out of this jam. If society wanted to fix this horrific crime against ordinary humanity, we would have had to demand more from our leaders than platitudes. But society didn't and that is how we stumbled into our present reality of Brexit and Donald Trump.

Every day, on the deserted beaches of Albufeira in the desolate month of January 2010, I walked alone in dread and fear for today's generation. In between the crashes of the Atlantic's winter surf, I felt the tide of my own sad history drag me under its strong current. I couldn't shake the realisation that history was repeating itself and that I didn't have an abundance of time to sufficiently warn people of the dangers that lay ahead for our world if we didn't fight against the forces who would use this crisis to eradicate the welfare state.

My past life kept rolling in and it always came back to my childhood and places like Sowerby Bridge.

My mum tried to paint our move to Sowerby Bridge as a step up but in many ways, like our move to Bradford, this was another step down towards our doom rather than salvation.

She'd rented a desolate outbuilding on a small farm that seemed to be located on the highest hill in the town of Sowerby Bridge. It was more horrific and primordial than our previous doss. The outbuilding had been converted two decades before our arrival into a primitive cottage for a farm labourer and his family. As the last occupant had recently committed suicide by hanging himself on a metal hook that jutted out high on the entrance wall, the farm owner was willing to rent it to my mother at an affordable rate. Each time I came back from school or work to these spartan quarters, I stared up at that hook and thought of the man hanging lifeless by the front door and how hopeless my existence felt to me. The cottage was made out of hard cold stone and lacked gas lighting, so we relied upon cheap candles to keep darkness at bay in the evening. It felt like we were living in an unfriendly cave.

It was not comfortable in that cottage and Bill's rage at society for making him live in the 'bloody muck' of that dismal, squalid place made sure there was no love in our new home. He was always drunk and as we could rarely afford a proper ration of coal the hearth was at most times cold. So, our bones were perpetually damp from a cold draught that slipped in under the door and burrowed deep into our blood like a termite drives through wood. We were hungry and our moods perpetually on edge because we didn't know what real or imagined slight would set Bill off on a tangent of violent anger.

The threat of Bill's violence hung in the air like thunder in a humid afternoon summer sky. In that barren cottage, I always felt apprehensive, nervous, hungry and sickly. My skin began to ache from both chilblains and boils. Every day at school or work, I dreaded the evening to come because I knew that the night time never promised quiet, only rage from Bill and trepidation from the rest of us.

At teatime each night, Bill would eat the greatest portion of our meal. He'd wash it down with rum bought at the off licence on his way back from his shift at the rendering plant. As we had no glasses, Bill would drink from a jam jar and with his other hand roll a cheap, coarse tobacco cigarette that he lit with a match that he struck off the sole of his boot. At the start of his drinking session, he would sing sea shanties that he had learned in the Navy during the First World War.

But as the evening progressed the songs became darker, and when he stopped singing to speak his voice was slurred from drink and bellicosity. With each swig from his jam jar, it was like watching a timer count down to an explosion.

Not long after our tea, my sister and I would depart to our bed in the room upstairs where, with flickering light from a candle, I'd either try to read from a library book or talk with my sister about what our lives would be like once we had grown up and were free from our mother and her man Bill.

By the time we had nodded off to sleep in each other's arms to keep warm, Bill's anger would begin to stir like a tiger looking for prey.

Always at around 10 p.m. we'd awake to the sound of Bill's voice made acrimonious by drink. My sister and I would hear my mum try to calm his anger with kind words that moved to pleading and then begging. It rarely succeeded because Bill's grievances weren't rational; it was rage that came from deep inside him. He felt that society had failed him, let him down: 'Since the end of bloody war, they gave us who served the King nowt.' It wasn't that he was wrong, it was that Bill struck out both physically and verbally at those who weren't responsible for the Great War, the

Depression, the hunger of our class and the entitlements of the elites. He just abused what was nearest and most vulnerable to him and that happened to be my mum.

I know that if Bill were alive today, he'd have voted Brexit because his inclination was to look for easy scapegoats for his problems and those of Britain. He didn't think deeply about his circumstances and never trusted politicians. He only gave vent to his hatred and in later years, try as I might to explain to him the changing face of Britain, he would have none of it. Like people today talk of the 1950s, Bill talked of the glorious past before the war with the Kaiser, 'when things were right with the world'.

His yelling would reach its crescendo with a terrible ferocity. My sister and I would hear the few sticks of furniture that the cottage possessed being hurled about the kitchen. We'd hear our mum trying to defend herself from him with either reasonable words or defiant invective. Invariably, in mid-sentence, my mum was silenced with a punch and then she would cry out in both pain and terror.

If the beating persisted my sister and I would rush from our bed to the kitchen and try our best to protect our mother from her boyfriend's violent physical outbursts. Once downstairs, we'd see Bill in the flickering candlelight attacking our mum with his fists while lashing her with vile obscenities that questioned her loyalty to him.

Even now, after so many years have passed – a lifetime – and with my mum long dead, those images of her being hit and trying to fight off her attacker disturb me profoundly.

They always make me feel, even though I was a child, like I didn't adequately protect her.

When Bill beat our mother, my sister and I tried at first to separate him from our mum by taunting him like one would a bear that was mauling its victim. When that failed, we'd jump on his back and try to slap his face with our small hands to make him stop hurting. It always failed. His shoulder had been injured in the First World War, and we soon learned that if we applied the right pressure it would dislocate, which immediately stopped him from causing further harm to our mum. Once that was done, Bill would scream out like the Cyclops blinded by Ulysses and proceed to stumble around the room until, exhausted from the drink, his anger and the pain from the dislocated shoulder, he'd fall to the floor beside our mother. As the adrenalin ebbed away from me and my sister, we'd find ourselves crying and calling out for our dad. But he wasn't there and never would be again. So, Alberta and I would also crumple in surrender to the hard stone floor, exhausted, frightened and terribly alone. After a while, silence overcame us all and we'd lie on the cold floor gradually becoming still.

The images I have of austerity in the 1930s are of hunger, filth, fear, violence, death and an overwhelming sadness. I know austerity is not any kinder to its victims today than it was in my time. Spouses are still being beaten; children are witness to violence and being abused by adults. This comes not because humans are inherently cruel but because once their dignity is stolen by poverty, they can lose their humanity. Austerity both then and now breeds inhumanity in those affected by it.

Bill's actions against my mum will always be inexcusable. But had not the conditions of poverty, precarious work and the shellshock of war not scarred his spirit, perhaps he would have been a kinder man to both others and himself. In later life, he shed most of his violent tendencies when he found steady work at the cat's-eye factory in Halifax. His temperament changed when he had enough to not only pay his rent for a tenement house but afford a week's vacation for my mum and him every year at Bridlington. Most of his cruelty abated when the 1945 Labour government enacted fair working conditions. He was content to work, watch football at Halifax's Shay stadium on Saturday afternoons and tend to his allotment patch in summer. In fact, in the late 1950s when they were both nearing sixty, he wed my mother in secret to ensure she had the right to receive his pension upon his death. Up until then, they'd lived as common law man and wife but both friends and neighbours assumed they were married. It was a deception used to prevent my mum having to explain how her relationship with Bill condemned my father to rough living after he had been cast adrift from our dosshouse in St Andrew's Villas.

Life, at the best of times, is complicated but during a universal crisis like the Great Depression many people stepped outside of the line of what was decent or civilised. In 2017, because of austerity, that is happening again and it will cause permanent emotional damage to another generation.

History is repeating itself but it is not coming back as farce but retribution for our own irresponsibility at not defending our stake in a just society.

In many ways, this low-wage economy is just as unsettling for a worker as mass unemployment was to my father's generation. There is no question that low wages, just like no wages, leave an individual prone to anxiety and feeling like the state just isn't looking out for their best interests. Moreover, the lower the wages the more an individual must rely upon a government to supplement their toil. Considering that zero-hour contract work increased by 20 per cent from 2015 to 2016 and now accounts for how one million workers earn their pay, low wages are here to stay. Moreover, agency work has increased by 30 per cent since 2011 and now almost 900,000 people are employed through third-party agencies. This may be an efficient way to handle human resources for an employer but the person on contract earns on average £460 less per year than a counterpart hired without an agency contract.

In-work poverty is becoming a norm for many workers, much like it was for unskilled labourers in the 1920s and 1930s. The Rowntree Foundation did a study in 2016 that determined that the housing crisis has helped push 13.5 million people into poverty. The Foundation determined that these people spent 60 per cent of their incomes or benefits on housing and therefore were well below the poverty line. But what is very disturbing is that of those 13.5 million people, 7 million (55 per cent) were poor even though they were in full-time work. In-work poverty that reaches into the millions tells me that the Tories' mantra that full-time work leads to prosperity is a sham. Moreover, it indicates that the Tories' living wage is also a deception because, if it were truly a living wage, then there would be no poverty for those in work. Most importantly, in-work poverty also proves that removing low-income workers from the tax rolls without relief on the cost of housing, heat, transport or food is just a diversion to excuse tax cuts to the wealthy.

When you have such a large contingent of people who are punching the clock but still struggling to make ends meet, it is clear that both David Cameron's coalition government and now Theresa May's majority government have done enormous harm to our society. By privatising social services, weakening the NHS, providing tax cuts to the rich and not implementing a real living wage they have broken a covenant between government and the people that democracy should work for all, not just entitled special interest groups.

It does not surprise me that a report by the think-tank Centre for Cities concluded in a 2016 study of wages and welfare that a majority of cities in the north and the Midlands were afflicted by a greater amount of their population struggling on low pay. The paltry pay packets are compelling these workers to be reliant on in-work welfare benefits that, thanks to George Osborne's 2016 Budget, are diminishing with the same haste as glacial ice in Greenland. I have known since I was in short pants that the north and other areas of Britain rarely get a fair deal from Westminster because we have always been treated like our colonies once were: as places to exploit rather than to invest in. It is outrageous that in the twenty-first century the government is still talking about building a northern powerhouse but never gets any closer to completing it.

The simple fact is that, if you don't reside in the Home Counties, your postcode is unimportant to the Tories except for the raw materials that their corporate mates can extract from the land to enrich the wealthy who reside in the south. As long as Tories govern, there will be no northern powerhouse, and no improved economic deal for Scotland and Wales to control their social destiny. In fact, the only way that Britain can become a truly equal state is by introducing proportional representation into its voting act and making our nation a true federation like Canada or the cantons of Switzerland. Moreover, if power isn't devolved within the next few years, it is unlikely that the union will be able to withstand both Brexit and austerity.

Right now, Britain stands on a very unsteady rope bridge that spans a deep gorge created by globalisation and the pursuit of low taxes for the wealthy. The International Finance Corporation (IFC) predicts that wage growth for ordinary workers over the next decade will be the worst Britain has seen in seventy years because of Tory austerity and the Tories' mishandling of the Brexit crisis. Britain doesn't have a moment to lose if it wants to prevent the social tragedies my generation encountered growing up to befall their children.

As for today's housing crisis, it mirrors the trouble families like mine endured before the welfare state because the young, poorly paid and unemployed cannot find decent, affordable accommodation. Brexit happened because too many people feel that they have been left behind when it comes to wages and a decent standard of living, and they were fooled into thinking that the cure was leaving the EU and did not understand that only trade unionism and progressive governments can provide the environment for a better standard of living.

During our exile in Sowerby Bridge I was far removed from politics – I wasn't even able to see a movie matinee. Anyway, there was no need for newsreels to teach me about the politics of tyrants because my mum, sister, little brother and I lived under the roof of a domestic dictator. I learned to avoid home as much as possible but that was not too difficult because I had found part-time work during the evenings and weekends, delivering coal on a cart pulled by a wizened old horse. I worked with a man who had been injured down in the mines and, because of his lameness, I did most of the physical work. So, I didn't have much time to contemplate the world outside of my small focus. If I wasn't at school, I was shifting hundred-weight coal sacks to customers through the villages that dotted the rough West Yorkshire hills. It was punishing work for an eleven-year-old boy but all I had known was labour since I was seven. I did, however, once again realise that not all children were forced into servitude because, when I delivered these giant sacks of coal, sometimes I caught sight of children my age studying piano inside their homes.

The books that I was beginning to read at the library reinforced my street knowledge of injustice. My sister used to find it very funny that I read by torchlight late into the night and would wake bleary-eyed for school. She didn't understand that the more I read, the more I felt like I was far away from the tragedies that seemed to have swallowed up our future. My sister was already fourteen so she was in full-time employment in a mill in Halifax and would say, 'I've got no time for books, Harry. They're for rich folk, not bread and dripping folks like us.' By that age, my sister already had a worn beauty about her because of what had happened in our childhood. Boys were chasing her and she was chasing them back, but that was because she, like my mother before her and most working-class women of that era, had no escape from the drudgery of their lives except through marriage, which rarely proved happy.

Once, I saw her in the distance pressed up against a piss-stained wall in a back alley with a boy much older than her fourteen years. Later on, I asked her what she had been doing with the boy. 'Having a fuck, it's what all the girls do,' was her reply to me.

Within a year, Bill had been fired from his job at the rendering plant and we moved with him to nearby King Cross, Halifax. My sister looked at me and said, 'As soon as I get the dosh, I'll move out on my own. I can't stand Mum and her pig man.'

Chapter Ten:
The Threat to Civilisation

During the 1930s, debt roared like an unsettled ocean behind my family's hurried footsteps as we flitted from neighbourhood to neighbourhood either in search of work or on the run from bad debts to landlords. That tsunami of financial disquiet never really grew still for my kind until after the war, when Attlee's Labour government introduced housing, wage and education policies that benefited every citizen.

Until that time, there was nowt for us and most of the citizens of our nation. There was never enough money for the rent, for the coal, for the gaslight, for food or for clothes. In or out of work, it was a battle that was designed to be like the curse of Sisyphus where you struggled eternally and never got ahead. It is not any different for ordinary people today because wages don't cover the cost of living any more. Britain hasn't seen so much unsecured personal debt sprawling across the ledger books of ordinary people since 2008. Then we were at the height of the banking crisis and now we are still in its wake because the crisis was mishandled, which allowed for the out-of-control housing bubble to balloon, making ordinary but decent accommodation far more expensive than it should be.

Everything a normal household needs to improve their lot is out of their reach; even the soaring cost of train travel limits access to the well-paid jobs and post-secondary education that give an individual a chance to move up the rungs of society. If we are not careful, soon our healthcare will be out of the reach of many because it will be monetised by the hedge funds. Our whole economy is driven by debt because our governments don't want to address the inadequacies of ordinary wages even with in-work benefits. But we must begin to have that discussion because when top executives in this country make 120 per cent more than their average employee, democracy starts to capsize.

Over my lifetime, I've seen too many bubbles burst that were inflated by the greed of some but whose cost was always borne by those who could least afford it. Like in the Great Depression, the ordinary people of today were made to pay for the malfeasance and greed of our bankers and hedge-fund managers who caused the 2007–8 banking fiasco.

It's why democracy and our civil society are so grievously threatened by populism, which feeds off legitimate grievances but produces small-mindedness and hate. Yet while populism builds its political army of resentment, mainstream politicians appear to be as ossified as the Ancien Régime of France in the eighteenth century in their response to it. We must fight back against malevolent forces with the same passion as my generation attacked and defeated Nazism. We must combat the nefarious beliefs UKIP espouses about immigration, as well as the Tory erosion of good government through castigating the poor to protect the inherited wealth of the rich, in the same manner as my generation defeated a thousand years of feudalism in Britain at the end of the Second World War. We voted for change, we demanded change and we held our government to account until change was made to our communities. We didn't sit idly by; we pitched in to make sure that politics would never again be the exclusive province of the 1 per cent.

Right now, the young, middle-aged and old must return to politics by joining political parties that they feel best match their ideals. And they must also commit themselves to attending meetings conducted by their local party organisations. They need to express their views and learn the opinions and ideas of other members. Everybody who is of voting age must go out and vote and ensure that their friends, neighbours and even strangers do the same. Moreover, if you are a member of a trade union, you must become an engaged member by joining committees, learning about the politics of trade unionism or assisting with the many philanthropic activities that trade unions engage in, from food banks to helping newly arrived refugees. If you are not affiliated to a union, become involved with those who seek to remedy homelessness and hunger in your neighbourhood by joining a nonprofit group. Life cannot just be about your family or your leisure activities; it must be about putting back into your community and country through being an engaged participant in democracy, which also means spending time each day to consider the news and how it relates to you.

Our ability to combat austerity and the growing authoritarianism of our politics at home and abroad can only begin when we as individuals take the time to care about our communities.

It was such a long time ago, but I still remember many of the people I rubbed shoulders with in my adolescence, during my war service and in my middle age who shaped the way I see the world today. Many of those people taught me life lessons that I have retained all through my days. They made me a better person and a more engaged citizen. I will never forget them until the candle of my life is extinguished and nor should you forget those who have influenced and shaped the good you have done while on this earth.

When I think of my childhood I see it as an endless circle of bus rides and bus stops that took my family into different villages, towns and cities, each place more desperate than the last: Barnsley, Bradford, Sowerby Bridge, King Cross and, finally, Boothtown Road in Halifax. At each place, something was always lost: my sister Marion dead in Barnsley and my father Albert abandoned in St Andrew's Villas.

For a while in King Cross, we even lost our mum when her boyfriend Bill's new venture went stale even before it really began. Bill took us to King Cross, a neighbourhood that hung on to the outskirts of Halifax like ash on a chain-smoker's cigarette, because his opportunities were limited in Sowerby Bridge after he lost his job. He gambled that his fortunes might change if he opened up a modest butcher's shop in a run-down neighbourhood. So, in the dead centre of its penury, Bill nailed up his shingle on a shop that sat squat in an alley of tumbling-down buildings that looked more medieval than twentieth century. At its back, there was a canal, which Bill used like a toilet to dispose of the bits of intestine, brain and waste that even a hungry man would turn his nose up at. As his speciality was low-grade meat of dubious provenance made to measure for the ill shod, Bill believed he might make a modest income. However, not long after he opened for business, Bill was packing up the shop because he lacked both capital and entrepreneurial acumen; he just couldn't survive when the few customers he had required credit to make their orders and so he went bust.

Having no prospect of work and debts mounting up, Bill was terrified and, as he was a bully, he took out his fear violently on my mum. After a particularly nasty row that included throwing a chair against a wall, he stormed out of our tenement house saying he was done with my mum and her menagerie of bairns. Were it not for the fact that my sister was working full-time in a Halifax mill and I was working part-time, we would have been homeless in short order. Losing the one thing that gave my mother the aura of working-class respectability, a man in employment who she could pretend was her husband, quickly caused her to spiral downwards, mentally, physically and emotionally.

But there was another reason for her distress at Bill's departure: as his final parting gift, he'd made my mum pregnant at the age of forty-one.

During those first few months of pregnancy, before her belly showed, my mother plotted, planned and raged against her lover. In the end, fearful of rearing a child in very late middle age without financial prospects, my mother took desperate and irrational measures. She decided to leave my sister, me and our baby brother to our own devices and search for Bill in Bradford, where rumour had it he had returned to work again as a pig man. In tears, our mum told us, 'I'll be gone for a while to find our Bill.' Taking some savings from my sister, our mother departed with a promise; she would write to us of her endeavours to recapture Bill. Her letters during her absence were sporadic but, somehow, my sister and I were able to hold together our household.

As it was still the Depression and we lived in a degraded part of town, no one questioned why we lived without our parents. For months, we didn't see our mum and in many ways we were happier as our lives were less tempestuous. She finally returned in spring 1935 with her new son in her arms and Bill.

He proved on his return to be less violent towards our mother. Perhaps becoming a father again at so late a stage in his life had tamed him; or perhaps it was the fact that he quickly found steady work at a butcher's shop in Halifax, which paid not well but decently enough for the era. By 1937, Bill, for the first time in his life, felt like he was putting down roots. He could afford small extra luxuries from his take-home pay, including an antiquated wireless that was powered by wet batteries that had to be taken to a shop to be recharged. To Bill, the fact that he had the dosh to afford a primitive radio and the leisure to listen to football matches and drink a beer in a sparsely decorated sitting room meant that he had come out well from the Great Depression. Every time Bill switched on the wireless and the tubes inside its wooden box hummed to life allowing voices to stumble out of the speaker like the genie from the lamp, he'd remark, 'It's bloody magical.'

Even before Bill had the dosh to afford to buy a radio, I was discovering the world was becoming more unhinged by the politics of nationalism. Mussolini was arresting and torturing communists, democrats and anyone who opposed his fascist rule. Hitler in Germany was ferociously making Jews unwelcome in their own country while, bit by bit, he tore up the Treaty of Versailles and reabsorbed territory that had been occupied by the French after the First World War. At the pictures, when the newsreels flashed across the screen, I saw Hitler's blackshirts march with menace in Germany while El Duce's air force bombed Abyssinia with poison gas. Fellow cinemagoers were appalled and frightened in the same way that Assad's bombing of Aleppo shocks and horrifies today's armchair spectators of war.

As the world stumbled towards another armed conflict that would be far worse than the last conflagration, there were show trials in Russia, revolutions in the Balkans, disquiet in Spain and a brutal war being waged by Japan in China. At home the *Daily Mail* complained about the scourge of Jewish refugees from Germany, and politicians wanted Britain to believe that they were desperate to get to Britain not from fear of Hitler but out of desire to subvert our way of life through their foreign ways and Bolshevik tendencies. If this doesn't remind you of Donald Trump, then you have not been paying attention to his speeches for the last two years.

Despite my young age, I understood instinctively what was happening to Europe because my soul had been made old from the hardships and cruel civic education of the Great Depression. With dread, I knew that the dark events that swirled around Europe and the world were about to impact not only my life but everyone else negatively.

Even in Halifax, so removed from the world at large, people's conversations were heavy with fear about what was transpiring in the world. It was only natural that those older than me were worried about another war coming or that the austerity they had known since 1929 would never end. We have these same misgivings today when we see the sabre-rattling of Putin in Russia or the Chinese government stretching their might out across the waters that surround Asia. Where does it end, we ask, when Donald Trump in his tweets tries to provoke the insane dictator of North Korea, Kim Jong-un, to make good on his promise to build a nuclear missile capable of reaching the Californian coast even though the nuclear Armageddon clock is at three minutes to midnight?

When I turned thirteen in 1936, I had only one year left of school and I was frightened. I realised my future had few prospects because I couldn't follow my father into his career. I knew that, without family connections or education, the economics and politics of the 1930s left me with limited prospects much like many young people today.

In my last days as a schoolboy, I didn't have grand aspirations. I was working class despite the poetry and novels I read in my leisure time, and I was aware that I wasn't made for anything other than hard physical work, which I had been doing since the age of seven. I just wanted a chance to find a decent working-class profession that would keep me from living on the streets. I wanted ordinary things to come my way, like a girlfriend, a decent place to kip and the promise that when I got older I'd have sufficient resources to marry and make a family of my own that would live in a proper house where food and heat were never rationed. I knew that wasn't too much to demand from my country. But I didn't even think I could attain that because there was a serious question as to whether I'd get a school leaving certificate.

No matter how hard I worked at my part-time job, there hadn't been enough to afford a pair of shoes for that winter. I was reduced to trying to patch my old ones with newspaper and cardboard but, when the bottoms fell apart, I stopped regularly attending school. I was ashamed and humiliated and didn't want to listen to the taunts from other students who had more resources but less humanity. Not attending gutted me because I did enjoy my lessons and I felt less than useless. My maths teacher noticed my absence and, because he was a decent man who was disgusted by how our country sacrificed young men in needless battles and children in economic depression, he helped me.

One day when I did turn up, he asked me to stay after class. I believed I was about to get a caning for my absences but instead he presented me with a new pair of shoes. 'Not a word to anyone else,' he said to me while he took a snuff box from his worn suit jacket. This teacher didn't want a fuss made over something that he thought should be second nature to any civilised person, but his act of kindness allowed me to continue my schooling and leave school at fourteen with my certificate.

Today, many school teachers are compelled to show similar acts of kindness to vulnerable students in their classrooms by quietly ensuring they have proper winter jackets, shoes or food. Schools funds are so truncated that teachers are buying school supplies out of their own pockets. However, teachers in rich postal codes never need to worry about providing books or clothing for their students because, like in the ancient days of my youth, the well-off always take care of their own first.

It's why when Theresa May, during her 2017 New Year's address to the nation, spoke about bringing more social equality to Britain, I didn't believe her. 'Cobblers,' I said to myself. Our present government is too obsessed by Brexit, third runways at Heathrow or grammar schools to tackle the root causes of our society's misfortunes. This present-day Tory administration is as horribly and dangerously separated from the needs of the people as their party was in the early twentieth century. But back then my generation did have one advantage over today's dispossessed; we knew the enemy to our success wasn't the unionised worker but those who sought to never pay a decent wage to their employees. We knew our enemies were politicians and governments that sought to maintain their privileges over the interests of the common people.

It's like colour blindness, but many today don't see that their political enemies are those at the top, not those who dwell down below them. The reason why so many of our fellow citizens don't see this is because the return of poverty and economic inequality evolved so gradually over the last three decades that few took notice of it. Inch by inch, year by year, like sea levels from global warming, poverty has risen since Margaret Thatcher swung her political wrecking ball against the welfare state through deregulation and privatisation. And now, we are at a point in our history that hasn't been this perilous for both peace and prosperity since the days just before the Second World War.

To prevent my past becoming your future, the majority of our citizens must become not only politicised but also humanised by the suffering they see all around them. Empathy must return to our shores – not the knee-jerk sympathy an individual sad tale in the tabloids evokes but a natural connection to other human beings. We must become like we were in the years between 1939 and 1945: larger than our own personal desires.

After I finished my schooling, my sister took me to Blackpool as a leaving gift and said, 'This is the last day you will be a boy, so let's enjoy it and ride the dodgems until our money runs out.'

Soon after, I started work as a grocer's assistant for a shop located in the Halifax arcade. I told myself that I'd be damned if I let any government or society treat me in the same way they had my father. I worked hard and on most days put in a ten- to eleven-hour day. My employer was good to me, or as good as I was ever going to get during a time when there were next to no labour laws. With my spare wages, I spent some, as all young people do, on entertainment. I'd enjoy a pint with friends I'd made in Halifax and sometimes I went to the pictures with a girl or to a dance hall to listen to live jazz music and forget that I didn't have many prospects in life.

I was aware my education was spotty and it shamed me. It made me have a burning desire to improve myself. I wanted to know how to fight back against those forces in our society that made my family and the working class go hungry for almost a decade in Britain. I was angry and I wanted to get even. So, I signed up for courses at a co-operative learning academy where I took elocution lessons and also courses in English literature and history. When I began to take guitar lessons from a veteran of the Spanish Civil War, I started to appreciate that no one was safe from fascism. My teacher was now a refugee and was married to a British woman. In between teaching me how to play my chords, he taught me about socialism, the fight against General Franco and the loneliness of exile. Over the months that I studied with him, I never got very good at the guitar but I did become proficient in the knowledge that, as sure as winter follows autumn, the dogs of war were about to be unleashed on my generation.

During one of my last lessons with my guitar teacher, he said to me, 'In this life you have to make a stand for what you think is right, no matter how frightened you may be, because the real terror comes in doing nothing. Best be prepared because a terrible war is coming. It's going to upend civilisation like an earthquake topples great and ancient cities.'

Chapter Eleven:
War and the Rebirth of Britain

On 1 September 1939, the carefree days of summer ended in an unrelenting shower of blood when Hitler's forces charged across the Polish countryside. I was sixteen when Prime Minister Chamberlain addressed the nation on the wireless and said that we were in a state of war with Germany. The peace that had held since 1918 was extinguished like a cigarette under a moving foot. Nazi tyranny battered Europe like a powerful storm. The lights of civilisation flickered, dimmed and then died across the continent when Hitler turned his armies westward to consume Belgium, Holland and France by Blitzkrieg. Everyone knew that darkness would soon come Britain's way and there was little we could do to stop it because we were woefully unprepared for battle. City lights were gutted to prevent German bombers finding their targets down below, where we lived and worked. Even church bells were hushed because jubilation was on hiatus until the war was won.

In her hour of need, I didn't have any particular attachment to my country because I had seen her back turn on me and my kind when we also required salvation. 'Bugger you, Britain' was a phrase I never quite articulated out loud but held close to my heart.

I knew that war, like poverty, always consumes the weakest first so I felt some angst as to what was to become of me. I was afraid it might devour my manhood like the economic inferno of the 1930s had done to my childhood. But I was also aware that I had little choice over what the war would do to me because I was young and without influence.

It wasn't that I didn't realise that Hitler was evil – anybody who watched the newsreels or read the papers could see that. It's just his nefariousness didn't seem to excuse the manner in which Britain treated the working class, the poor and the vulnerable. Much later on in the war, when I was in Europe, I was shocked to see that most working-class neighbourhoods in Belgium and Holland were luxurious compared to the squalor workers were expected to call home in Britain. These places abroad even had indoor toilets, whereas we at home scrambled outside no matter the weather to do our business like animals. I thought if those countries could afford to treat their workers with more respect than ours, a mighty empire, then it meant our leaders and elite really wanted us to be subjugated.

The war asked much from everyone and many found these

demands, from identity cards, conscription and rationing to youthful mortality, hard to swallow. There was dissent, displeasure and outright hostility to the war by many because the Great Depression had exhausted the nation's patience with government. Too many lives had been sacrificed to austerity and that is why our acceptance of blackouts, state surveillance and eventually rationing was grudgingly given. We had no trust in our so-called betters after ten years of hunger, massive unemployment and horrendous living conditions.

Besides, the carnage that occurred in the First World War was fresh in the memory of many. When on my way to work at the Halifax arcade in the morning, I'd spy the glaring, bellicose headlines of our daily newspapers that were displayed in front of kiosks, I remembered the soldiers, broken by the First World War and impoverished by the Great Depression, who lived with us in the dosshouse in Bradford. They had taught me all too well that young men are sent to fight the battles of old men and are recompensed with either death or severe injury for their sacrifice to King and Country.

It wasn't until Churchill formed a coalition government in 1940 that people began to feel confident that their leaders were sincere in their aim to protect Britain. It wasn't so much Churchill being made Prime Minister that gave us this confidence, but that Labour would be an equal partner in his government, which buoyed our spirits. Still, many had lingering doubts. On many occasions down the pub I heard the whinge that it wouldn't be the toffs that won this war or gave their blood, sweat and tears to defend our island but the working class. That's why I always feel sardonic when present-day Tories encourage the country to gather the courage of my generation when it comes to the challenges we now face because of Brexit or international terrorism. You see, it's all a wicked deceit on their part to get people today to sign up to political decisions that are either dangerous or unhelpful to the majority of citizens. My generation only showed its mettle to defend Britain when the elites proved they were prepared to share the spoils of peace with us. Had they not, it is quite possible the war would have gone a different way.

The one lesson that the present generation can take from those who lived through the Second World War is to never surrender your future by putting your faith blindly in politicians. You must demand from government, as we did long ago, one concession: if you are to shoulder the burden to maintain this country's survival, you must share in the prosperity to come. Without such guarantees the present generation will be slaves to eternal political rhetoric that puts their concerns at the back of the queue.

I didn't feel beholden to Britain at the onset of war. How could I after the decade-long odyssey my family underwent across the Yorkshire landscape in search of food, work and secure housing? After so long living in the wilderness of society, I trusted neither politicians nor people of economic influence. I was resentful that my formative years had been spoiled by economic turmoil.

It seemed a bitter joke to me that when my family finally

arrived on some solid economic ground in Halifax, the tide of war was rushing in to wash it all away.

I didn't think I could escape the war but neither could anyone else regardless of what station in life they occupied. When I was given an opportunity by my employer, a prosperous Halifax grocer, to sit out the war by joining his Christadelphian sect and becoming a conscientious objector, I didn't take it, even though he had sugar-coated his request by promising me a third of his business upon his death. 'You've been a good manager to me and it would be a shame to lose your life in this war.'

The offer was tempting because, had I accepted, it would have guaranteed me the right to join the lower middle class. It certainly was alluring enough for his other two managers: they jumped at the chance to sit out the war and move up life's ladder. I declined not because I felt any affinity for my country but because my dad had taught me, in his quiet and kind way, that we must always do our best when it is a battle between good and evil. Besides, the last place I wanted to be in either war or peace was Halifax.

When France fell in the summer of 1940, Bill looked at me over our kitchen table and said, 'We're in the shit now, just like it's 1916 all over again. Best you start thinking, lad, of what you'll be doing in this bloody war and pray it's not going to be a meat grinder like the last one.'

Britain's cities were now clothed with sandbags and shrouded at night by the blackout. Far away from Yorkshire, the Battle of Britain was coming to its close while the Blitz against London and our other great industrial centres was only just beginning. It was an uncertain time. We didn't know if we'd be able to win this war or even fight to a draw, but the words of defeat were still hard to express. However, the questions always remained on our lips: What happens to us even if we win against Hitler? Will nothing change in our society? Will everything remain the same with the elites on the top and the rest of us scrambling at the bottom of their table for crumbs? Nobody who wasn't rich wanted that. We wanted things to change.

Those who controlled the levers of society had not shared the burden of austerity they'd imposed upon the country during the Great Depression. It seems all so similar to today's crisis of faith in government. Many feel in this day and age that, while institutions like the NHS are within a hair's breadth of insolvency because of underfunding, they are bearing the brunt of Tory austerity without any recompense. And they are not wrong because even under austerity British executives make so much more than the average worker. Yet during the Second World War, to offset perceptions of a have and have-not society, the war-time government imposed an income tax of 95 per cent on top earners so that it would at least appear that they could not profit from the war.

While arguments raged in the House of Commons, at the bus queue, at the supper tables or down at the pub about military preparedness, the full impact of war drew closer to Britain. All of Europe was either under the control of Hitler's armies or neutral to our survival. Air raids spread death up and down the country. Germany's Luftwaffe was targeting our food supply through both the Battle of the Atlantic and the bombs that fell overhead on to us. As I was still too young, at seventeen, to join the services, I became an air-raid warden for my grocery company's warehouse, which stood on top of a moor that overlooked our town. I was provided with a tin hat from the First World War and sand buckets to fight any fires that might break out from an air raid. On my shifts, I'd look up into the night sky that was punctured by the pin pricks of starlight and try to spot malevolent Henkel bombers swarming towards their prey. I was playing toy soldiers and I knew these games of silly buggers would soon be replaced with the real thing for me and my friends.

One by one, as our eighteenth birthdays approached, we made our decision as to what branch of the services we would join. My friend Roy, who was six feet tall and had not been touched by the ravages of the economic downturn, chose the Guards because, as he told us, he wanted to fight the Hun. My friend Eric was less certain about the war and quite pleased that his trade as a tool- and die-maker allowed him to be deemed part of essential war work, which meant he was not required to join the forces. As for me, I knew only one thing: I wasn't going to go out of my way to die for my country, after what it had done to my kind for generations.

My initial feelings weren't unusual – they were the norm. The distrust of government was so strong that our politicians were afraid that the working class might not give 100 per cent for the war effort. That is why the Conservative, Labour and Liberal parties in the coalition government agreed that, after the conflict, society would reflect the interests of all its citizens, and consequently commissioned the Beveridge Report.

When the Beveridge Report was tabled in the House of Commons in 1942, it proved to be a revolutionary document because it was a builder's plan for a post-war Britain where all facets of the nation shared in its wealth and its work. It demanded public healthcare, affordable housing and education for all its citizens. This report provided a reason – beyond blind patriotism – for the working class to defend Britain against Hitler: they were no longer just fighting to defend the entitlements of the elite, but for their own future.

Today, politicians from all sides of the House of Commons need to create a new Beveridge Report for the twenty-first century that addresses the great divide that now separates the top 10 per cent of wage earners from everyone else. It must look at ways to combat automation, the sharing economy, democratic decline and the erosion of state services. We need an honest report to determine how we can renew our society, neighbourhoods and democracy through investment in our citizens and infrastructures. If politicians don't initiate a new Beveridge Report, then it is up to the citizenry to compel them through either the ballot box or protest. Surely the time has come for one of the parties, in their general election manifesto, to pledge to change our nation by instituting a new social architect's guide for Britain.

While politicians planned for our brave new world after the war, I was ordered by the RAF to report for my square-bashing at Padgate in Lancashire in winter 1941. The day before I was to depart, I went to the neighbourhood baths and paid 50p for a soak in a private tub. I remember the luxuriousness of both the hot water and the privacy. As I lathered my body in the warmth of the water with soft soap, not the harsh soap I was used to at home, peace overcame my body and mind. Momentarily, I thought of my dad when he long ago scrubbed himself clean after a shift in the pits in a tin tub located near the stove in our kitchen. There was an ache in my soul from missing him, from losing a father and a comrade too early in my life. As I rose from the tub, pulled the plug and dried myself, I was apprehended by fear. I suddenly realised I didn't know what would happen to me in this war that I was about to join. I was petrified but the terror passed because I was young, and the thought of leaving Halifax, and Yorkshire, for the adventure of a new life was more enticing than the threat of my extinction.

The next morning, my mum made me a breakfast of fresh bread slathered with rationed butter and homemade jam that she had saved for this occasion. In haste I tucked in because I was excited about this new venture I was about to undertake. I wanted to close the door on my old life as quickly as possible and begin this one. Yet the possibility of death toyed with my emotions as I drank my tea and ate my breakfast for the last time as a civilian.

The Great Depression had strained my relationship with my mother. Sometimes, we had rows where we used words like they were lances at a joust to the death. Since Bradford, our affection for each other was in short supply because resentment trumped endearment. But on that morning, before I left, I detected in my mum's hug an enormous energy of love for me. As we parted, my mum told me to be safe, and said, 'Don't go playing silly buggers, because life, Harry, is too bloody short by far. Come home in one piece and all will be right with the world.' As I walked away from our tenement home, my mum stood out on the stoop waving to me as she had once waved to my dad in Barnsley when he returned from his shift down at the coal face.

As the cold winter air scratched at my face, I understood that the trials and tribulations of my youth growing up poor in Great Depression Britain had come to a close. Now I was a man who had taken the King's Shilling. But I had done it not to defend the old order but hopefully, if I survived, to see a new world born out of the ashes of inequity.

I walked away from my house carrying a cardboard suitcase that contained some clothes, an Everyman's edition of Wordsworth's poetry, Dickens's *A Tale of Two Cities* and George Orwell's *Homage to Catalonia*. I had also brought with me a notebook, which I'd resolved to write in every day.

At the railway station, I waited for my train that would take me to the war. It was damp and cold and the platform

189

was deserted except for me and another man who was in his fifties whistling the tune 'Run Rabbit Run'.

The war and the threat of national annihilation broke down class barriers. Everything was more intense, visceral and meaningful during the struggle against fascism. Life was lived on the edge and that meant that every activity you did, from smoking a Capstan cigarette in a busy London street to kissing a woman in a crowded theatre, felt significant because it might be your last. Death waited for each one of us around every bend in the road, so our perceptions of what we wanted if we survived until peace returned had changed. Now, we knew that we didn't just want the platitudes of politicians, we wanted action. We wanted our nation to have more meaning than an empire and wealth for the few. We wanted to face the twentieth century with the confidence of democracy and the compassion of socialism. We wanted our lives to be free of want, ignorance and sickness. In short, we wanted what any human should want and deserve: a chance to grow old and add to the sum of life.

The war for me was not sorrowful like my boyhood growing up in the slums of Yorkshire. My war was good because I walked away from it after four years of being on the periphery without the need for even a sticking plaster. In many ways, the war, and my time in the RAF, was a profound spiritual and educational experience for me. I was able for the first time to live in close quarters with many unique and socially different individuals while being stationed all across our country and then in the war zones of Europe. Hurt, mayhem and slaughter were always on the horizon like an approaching storm. But I had never felt so safe and secure in my life because I could trust those around me in my unit and I knew that, as long as I did my duty, I'd be fed, clothed and given a bed to rest my head. I revelled in the anonymity of my blue serge uniform that defined me not by my class but by my service to my country. Wearing it sheared me of the enormous poverty of my background and, within the RAF, I was respected for the job I did and not because of my accent or background.

Before the war, my life was a compass point that never wavered further than fifty miles from Barnsley, the town of my birth, like it had been for all of my ancestors for the last 500 years. Yet when I joined the RAF to do my very small bit, I travelled the length and breadth of our country and much of Europe, which broadened my perception of humanity and our nation. I encountered air raids in London, where I felt the terror of indiscriminate death rain down. With my unit on training exercises, I marched across moors, fields, rivers, mountains and coastlines and, along the way, learned about the suffering and struggles of each region in both times of war and of peace. My time in the RAF taught me to love the people of my country for their unique cultures, different senses of humour and sensitive souls.

The men who shared my barracks, the brew-ups and piss-ups in unfamiliar towns added to my understanding of human nature and politics. In between arguments about football and discussions about girls, there was time to talk about the world and what we wanted from it after Hitler was done and dusted. Even some officers during and after the conflict were interested enough in me to lend me books on economics, history and literature. I met people from all walks of life in the RAF: the poverty-stricken, the working and middle class, the upper crust. The social barriers that had constrained people from mingling with other economic classes broke down as each year passed and the middle-class blokes who were in the services also recognised that Britain needed change.

For me, the moment I knew that Britain was changing for the better came during a brew-up in the countryside of Kent. A gramophone was taken out so that we could listen to music during our lunch and both working-class and middle-class lads had tears in their eyes when they heard Marian Anderson sing an aria from the opera *Samson and Delilah*. Listening to it, I knew that I was worthy of culture, education and love even though I was working class. Above us was blue sky and far off in the distance our armies battled through France and on to Holland, where we knew we were soon to travel. The war was all around us – even if death didn't come for us at this moment, it came for our mates who were serving in other branches of the military and it came for our family members who were killed in air raids or V1 bomber attacks.

It wasn't until the very end of the war that my unit was put to task overseas in the conflict zone, where I would serve as an RAF wireless op for a unit that was to be utilised to retrofit newly liberated Luftwaffe airfields in conflict zones.

When the final push against Hitler was on, my unit embarked for Europe in the belly of an ancient freighter that landed before sunrise in Ostend. We emerged from our hold just as day was about to break and glimpsed Europe smouldering from years of war. All around me was the smell of petrol and the aroma of fresh battles being waged nearby.

As our convoy lumbered across Belgium and Holland, moving from one damaged aerodrome to the next, I was confronted each day with the agony of war, the crime of war and its indiscriminate brutality. Europe had been turned into an ossuary; Hitler's scorched-earth policy had deliberately starved the people of Holland, who had lived off boiled tulip bulbs for their tea during the hungry winter. Humanity had fled the continent. As my unit followed behind our armies marching into Germany, Armageddon had writ his signature large over the landscape. Death, ruin and despair were everywhere, but trees had come to bloom in an early spring that caressed the misery all around us. Here in the rubble of Belgium and Holland, rich man, poor man, beggar man and thief had been marked a victim of this titanic battle against fascism.

As the last remnants of Hitler's armies held firm in an obliterated Berlin, my unit moved across the border between Holland and Germany in a convoy of American trucks. The totality of war's destruction littered the side of the road we took into northern Germany. Surrendered Wehrmacht soldiers marched to internment on one side while on the other side refugees from slave labour camps and eastern Prussia trudged with weary resolve to escape the conflict.

By the time we reached Hamburg, it was dusk and the scent of lilacs and death hung over the city like it was a corpse that had been left to rot in a field of flowers. From the back of a lorry, with a cigarette dangling from my lip and road dust caked on my face, I entered Germany's second largest city for the first time. It was a metropolis that had been eviscerated by the air war. It was Gomorrah, the day after Lot's wife had turned to stone, because it was a tomb to 50,000 civilians who had been killed in a three-day air raid that had evaporated over 10 square kilometres of its downtown core. Working-class districts, the port, thousands of apartments, shops, factories and schools were just heaps of rubble where people were still living like Neolithic humans in caves dug from the debris. We drove past the silhouette of its ruin in silence. We were dumbstruck by the power of modern war to obliterate an industrial cosmopolitan city and exile its citizens back in time to before the Middle Ages.

It would be another three days after we occupied Hamburg before Germany officially surrendered and peace once again held an uneasy dominion across Europe.

In that summer of occupation, I dusted off the debris of war, got my bearings and realised that I wasn't ready for civilian life just yet. It's why I signed on for several more years to be part of the occupational forces. The RAF had been good to me; it had taught me many things, helped me develop my self-esteem and learn to connect and interact with both my comrades and my peers. I was able throughout the horrors of that war to learn to love my fellow man again and even trust them with my hopes and desires. I had made good friends during my stint in the RAF but I also developed a better understanding of the other classes that made up Britain. It made me realise that not everyone who didn't come from the mean streets I'd inhabited as a child was an enemy. I realised that not everyone who hadn't got a raw deal during the Great Depression needed to be feared or loathed. I started to understand that my generation might be able to make a Britain where all of us could live and prosper together. It was under those conditions at the end of the war that a general election was called, with a vote to be held in July 1945.

I knew from the moment the election writ was dropped that it would decide my fate and the fate of my generation. From the year of my birth in 1923 to 1939, my life had been assailed by poverty, illness, a corrupt class system and the stress of living hand to mouth. I wanted it all to stop. I had experienced since childhood the brutality of poverty. I had seen how it abused and diminished those who lived under its sway. More lives had been lost to poverty from 1929 to 1939 than from all the battles our armed forces had engaged in on both the European and Asian fronts. My sister's death, our family being forced to abandon my dad, the hunger, the humiliation of debt and homelessness, the howls from cancer patients too poor to afford medicine, the charity Christmas meals for the indigent, the diving through rubbish bins for my tea . . . all came from a political and economic system that treated Britain's most vulnerable as chattel that had less value than livestock.

Labour's manifesto declared to all citizens of Britain that

> The nation wants food, work and homes. It wants more than that – it wants good food in plenty, useful work for all, and comfortable, labour-saving homes that take full advantage of the resources of modern science and productive industry. It wants a high and rising standard of living, security for all against a rainy day, an educational system that will give every boy and girl a chance to develop the best that is in them.

For me it was a pledge that I accepted as not only true but the inalienable right of my generation who had delivered victory to Britain in the war.

So when I stood in that queue to vote in the shadows of a ruined Nazi city, I was determined that this vote was my mark, my ascendency into a new society. My vote, I pledged, would give me a chance for both happiness and prosperity. It was an extraordinary election day because, while I voted in the charred remains of a German city for change in Britain, almost a million other servicemen and women were also voting while stationed in Europe, North America and Australia. Soldiers were even voting within earshot of battles being waged against imperial Japan.

When I made my mark for Labour that day, I wasn't just voting for myself. I was also casting a vote for my dead sister and father who lay nameless in paupers' pits. I was voting for all those who didn't survive the Great Depression or the war we had just fought. I voted for a future that guaranteed a right to housing, education and medical care regardless of your financial situation. I voted for an economy that was protected through the nationalising of key industries so that when industrial strategies were devised they would be for the benefit of the whole country, not just a select group of stockholders.

Casting a vote in that monumental election was my generation's chance to mark their X and claim their destiny from want, ignorance and ill health. It was electrifying and to this day the power of the ballot box to change society still sends shivers down my spine. The sheer joy, sense of power and feeling of being part of history have not died in me; the memory of the 1945 election shines bright and dims all the horrors that so many of us witnessed in the war and before. For me, the 1945 election will always be as joyous as a birth because it awakened in me the belief that the humblest of citizens' voices can be heard.

I still hear the echoes of those voices today in the protests of our young who demand a new and better deal for their generation or when they march against the creeping fascism of Donald Trump. Now, more than ever, we need to re-engage with democracy. Now, more than ever, we need people from all walks of life to make the sacrifice and join the honourable profession of politician before this craft becomes too polluted by the populism of Trump, Farage and Marine Le Pen. Now, more than ever, we need political parties that want to make their societies better for the common man and woman, not the top wage earners.

Chapter Twelve:
The Rationing of Happiness

The 1945 general election saw for the first time a government in Britain that was both of the people and for the people. It was extraordinary, but all the hope and promise they ignited in people like me didn't last. The pledge to make a better Britain based on practical socialism was eroded quickly through impatience, greed and self-interest. It began to expire after Attlee's government was forced to impose an extreme austerity, which covered the land like a hard frost, so that they could cover our war debts and build a sturdy welfare state.

For the first three years of austerity, I'd been immune to the hardships at home because I was still stationed with the occupational forces in Germany. In 1948 I returned to Britain with my German wife, whom I had wed the year previously in Hamburg. When I came home, I saw a nation humbled by peace because the wreckage from the Blitz still scarred London and we didn't have the money to clear it. Our country was as melancholic as a spinster living out her final years in a decrepit seaside boarding house. My return to Britain was a difficult transition for both myself and my new bride because, even though the welfare state was being built, there was not much sign of it in the north of England. In fact, Halifax, where we settled, looked far worse for wear than when I had left it in 1941.

At first, my wife and I moved into the unheated attic in my mum's tenement house, which was already full to capacity because my two younger brothers were still living there as well. As my mother had become embittered by much that had occurred in her life, she found it difficult to be civil to my new bride. So, with much acrimony, we moved on but, although jobs were plentiful, housing was not. At first the council wanted to settle us in the poor house because the great promise of new housing hadn't come to our part of Yorkshire. Naturally, it had been located in areas that had suffered the worst during the war, meaning the slums of my youth would have to wait a while longer to be cleared. However, before I was forced to lodge in the poor house, a friend of mine was able to put us up in her very small tenement home.

We, like everyone else, lived a beans-on-toast life. Austerity bathed our country in the sallow light that comes at the end of a grey wet afternoon. To my disappointment and anger, my wages just covered our rent, our food, a trip

200

to the cinema and a visit to the pub for a pint and Pimm's on Saturday nights.

Our spirits ached from the monotony of shortages in consumer goods, housing and entertainment. In those early days, most still had faith in Labour's bold initiative to build a green and pleasant land for all. Certainly, my faith was not yet shaken during those lean days when both meat and hope were a luxury, because I had experienced far worse heartaches as a bairn. Others, however, were less forgiving to Labour despite the many instances when their government had brought improvement to their ordinary lives.

I felt both pride and gratitude to the Labour Party for creating the NHS in 1948 because, by making healthcare a public rather than a commercial concern, it allowed me and millions of others to no longer fear that illness would lead to penury and homelessness. To this day, my gratitude to the Labour Party remains steadfast because it was they who emancipated our country from the shackles of pay-as-you-go healthcare.

No matter how much I could hear in the distance the sounds of the welfare state being constructed, it was also a time of despondency. Many believed we'd won the war but surrendered the peace to perpetual rationing, belt tightening and postponing personal pleasures for the national good. It was a fearful time to be young, middle-aged or old because none of us knew what tomorrow would bring. The Cold War was becoming more intense and nationalism was again rearing its head in the United States with its growing anti-communism.

In the 1950 general election, Labour polled over 1.5 million more votes than the Conservatives, but was returned to government with only a razor-thin majority of just six seats. This compelled Attlee to call another election in October 1951.

When the black autumn rains came to Halifax that year, the election was greeted with derision rather than enthusiasm from the voters. The damp had got into our hearts and no gas fire, finger of whisky or election slogans that proclaimed 'Yes everyone will be better under Labour' could extinguish the ache that each resident felt from ongoing rationing or undo how grim their lives had become since victory in Europe six years previously.

There was nowt in the shops, nowt in our larders, nowt in our hearts but unease, resentment and a sense that we'd been betrayed by our so-called betters. Simply going into a shop and seeing empty shelves made me realise that my city, my county, my country were a long way from the land of milk and honey that had been promised to us by Labour after the war. Simply put, the people had grown tired of sacrificing today for a brighter tomorrow.

During the general election in 1951, the newspapers, newsreels and wireless told us that the way we voted would determine how Britain would govern itself in the sunset of empire. It would decide once and for all whether Britain would remove the shackles of economic inequality that had blighted the prospects of millions of British citizens or if, in fear of the unknown, we would embrace a past that was ripe with nostalgia in the hope that we could rekindle our finest hour. Truly, it was a plebiscite on whether we could accept the hardships required to make Britain a democracy that functioned for everyone.

However, the mood in the country had chilled to Labour's earnest plans to transform Britain into a social democracy. We were as unhappy as those who voted for Brexit in 2016 because we saw no light at the end of the tunnel and Labour couldn't adequately explain to voters why we needed to live in this age of austerity. Even the most ardent believer in social justice can only live so long in the half-light of rationing and diminished expectations before umbrage takes hold of their better nature. It was just taking too long to change a thousand years of economic oppression for the ordinary voter. All they wanted was Technicolor to return to their humdrum lives, which began each morning with a cup of char and a slice of bread and jam made from turnips before they caught a bus to take them to work. My routine was no different than theirs: I punched a factory clock, worked a giant carpet loom and then eight hours later made my way home with other weary, drably dressed workers in Halifax's teatime light and returned to a cramped, uncomfortable flat. My wife and I were young but it seemed even to me the promise of peace had short-changed us. Like today, impatience and cynicism gripped the electorate.

At times, when I shaved to get ready to go down to the pub, the Tories' slogan to 'set the people free' was almost beguiling to me. But then I remembered what Tory policies had done to me and my family when we lived on poor relief and scrambled through rubbish bins looking for food. I remembered the squalor of my youth, so I was gratified that Labour had nationalised the railways, mines and steelworks, ensuring that many workers toiled under better conditions for more pay. I knew their good fortune would eventually come my way because the only real trickledown theory is when unions have power over many industries to elevate wages and improve working conditions.

Make no mistake, for most of us the early 1950s were a piece of cake in comparison to the meanness of the 1930s or the barbarity of the 1940s. Work was plentiful and great strides had been made to improve our society by the Attlee Labour government. So much good had been done through Clem Attlee's austerity and, because of it, we were given a decent and fair standard of living for over thirty years.

The same will never be said about David Cameron's new age of austerity that gutted welfare programmes and tightened the belts of the emaciated to allow corporations to gorge on cut-rate state asset sales like the Royal Mail. In 1951, austerity encompassed everyone but today it targets the wrong groups. As this modern austerity doesn't zero in on corporations, the wealthy or the middle class directly through tax hikes, it means that, until there is a change in government, we live with the continual diminishment of programmes that help young families, the mentally ill, school kids and senior citizens.

The Rationing of Happiness

In 1951, it was easy for most of us to forget all the good Labour had brought to Britain since the war because the daily battle for survival made us forget the bigger battles being waged to forge a better society and nation. On 18 October, Labour lost the general election to Winston Churchill. But even Churchill knew he could not put back the hands of time when it came to social housing, the NHS or the nationalisation of key industries. Labour's political revolution was so impressive that it lasted until 1979 when Margaret Thatcher began to dismantle the world my generation built for our children to live free of want.

Conclusion:

To Everything There Is a Season

I began this book when I was ninety-three and, as I finish it, I have just turned ninety-four. But I believe the seeds of this book were planted in me a long time ago when I was in my teens and I would ride my bike out to the moors near Halifax to be alone with my thoughts. There, I would put pen to paper to try to understand the injustices my family, my generation and my class endured because Britain was governed by and for elites. I wasn't radical then and I am not now but I knew that if you ignore the pleas of ordinary folk for good jobs, decent homes and a decent future, social unrest will soon follow. My long and generally happy and productive life only happened because the welfare state was created by a Labour government when I was twenty-two. It's why what I endured through my childhood is now a malevolent ghost that haunts my mind and will do so until I breathe no more.

I am an ordinary man who lived through extraordinary times. I am one of the last remaining voices from an era when Britain was savage and brutal to all those who did not have wealth.

Now when I shave in the morning and look at the skin on my face broken and cracked with age and my hands thin and frail, I wonder to myself what became of that young man who survived the Great Depression, and what happened to that Britain that delivered from the ashes of war peace and economic security to its citizens. The young man and Britain as a compassionate nation are no more.

Neo-liberalism has turned the welfare state into Bolton Abbey. It has become a beautiful pile of rubble. It was exposed to the indifference of successive governments, including Labour, for too long. Moreover, this generation has allowed the 1 per cent to steal its birth right and that can't continue for much longer without Britain returning to my past. And if we in the twenty-first century are forced to return to my past because the Tories have successfully murdered the welfare state, it will be more brutal and bloodier for you than it was for me so many years ago. This time there will be no mercy because the state will be able to monitor and control all facets of your life; our entire lives can be traced, from our use of mobiles and emails to comments on social media to purchases via credit card and the use of loyalty cards. Anonymity has gone, and the state has greater weaponry for social control than ever before. It will be impossible to resist and mobilise like we did in the 1930s and 1940s. You must begin to act now because tomorrow it could be too late.

Everything that we have today in terms of social benefits originates from those six years when Labour was in government after the war. Without the Atlee government, Britain would have been a dark and fearful place during the second half of the twentieth century. And yet many of our citizens are ignorant of history and made arrogant by the fake news of the right wing, which disparages the great accomplishments we made as a nation, when we cleared the slums, gave free healthcare to all, built affordable homes and made higher education accessible to working-class kids.

We shouldn't be where we are today as a people and as a society. A million people should not need to use food banks to keep their bellies full. Politics has failed the people and now too many are turning to right-wing populists the way the poor once flocked to snake-oil salesmen to cure their ailments. All our political parties are at fault and should be ashamed, but some are guiltier than others.

UKIP is a fraud. It can no more offer political salvation to the disenfranchised masses than a television evangelist can fast track you to heaven with a £100 donation to his dodgy ministry. And it is time the media and other political parties stopped paying lip service to their twenty-first-century variant of Mosley's fascism.

As for the Tories, their concept of aspirational politics is a cruel deceit. Toryism is no more than an elaborate pyramid scheme where they convince everyone to steal from the lowest to keep their place in the hierarchy.

As for Labour, my heart will always be with them, as it was even during the time of open civil war that occurred for the first two years of Jeremy Corbyn's leadership or when the Labour government pursued a war of dubious merit in Iraq. I hope that the party will heal its divisions and grow more united because of its recent electoral gains during the snap general election. But more importantly, I hope the party has learned it can't help the working classes, the vulnerable or the middle classes if the right wing and left wing of the party are at each other's throats in a blood feud. Perhaps since reducing Theresa May's working majority to a hung parliament in the election of June 2017, Labour politicians have learned to put their daggers down against each other and fight the true enemy of progress, the Tories. At any rate, it seems that after a long journey into a spiritual wilderness, Labour has been revitalised by its electoral success. Moreover, the success of Labour's 2017 election manifesto proves that pragmatic socialism is as attractive to this generation as it was to mine in 1945. Should Labour ever get a chance to unfurl this platform in a government for and by the people, Britain will have truly returned to the optimistic days of 1945 after Clem Attlee became Prime Minister.

We must never forget, nor deride or diminish, how much good New Labour did when in government. They established the minimum wage, greater environmental protection and greater inclusion, brokered the Good Friday Agreement and allowed for civil partnerships for gays and lesbians. Tony Blair and New Labour also were able to instil an optimism in our nation, which should not be discounted. But the sheer arrogance and folly of Iraq plus the financial obscenity of PFI, the private finance initiative that has indebted generations to come, left a bad taste in the mouths of many who believe in progressive politics. Up until the 2017 general election, many voters felt betrayed by Labour whether in Scotland, the Labour heartlands in England or the metropolitan regions – everyone had an axe to grind with Labour because they promised us the moon in the late 1990s and instead delivered us the shame of the Chilcot Inquiry. This has damaged the faith of many in Labour's ability to be a party for the worker, the middle class and the vulnerable. For most of the two years Jeremy Corbyn has been leader, he's had a difficult time trying to establish trust with the electorate for a variety of reasons, some of which are his fault and others the result of effective propaganda by those opposed to a more economically equal Britain. However, after Corbyn shattered the Tory party's fragile myth that they are a steady pair of hands in rough political seas in the 2017 election, his popularity has skyrocketed. But we should remember, if in time his appeal to the voter does plunge again, that it is not because he lacks competence or ideas, but because popularity for politicians is like the medieval wheel of fate perpetually turning.

To Everything There Is a Season

My faith in Labour has been tested over the years, but I have never doubted it is the only political movement in Britain that can deliver real change to ordinary people. That's why, in 2014, after years of being an anonymous citizen who went about his life trying to do the best for his family and community, I felt compelled to speak out about the decline of the welfare state and slow creep towards privatisation of the NHS, when I spoke at the Labour Party conference. My speech was shared almost 3 million times on Facebook because I was able to remind Britain that life before the welfare state and the NHS wasn't like an episode of *Downton Abbey* for the majority of citizens. I was able to talk of my sister's unjust death and of those who suffered from cancer but were denied morphine because they couldn't afford the cost of medicine. I was able to remind our nation of their ancestors' struggles. I was able to let people know that a nation can heal its injustices, its wounds and its animosity, if it has the courage to be a country that won't leave those wounded by austerity on the economic and social battlefields of life. I was honoured to speak for the dead of my generation and gratified that Labour in 2014 felt it was important to remind Britain of our inglorious past before the welfare state.

Under Corbyn, Labour has begun to show that it can harness the ideals of Clem Attlee's government, which won over working-class lads like me to the practical benefits that can be achieved by participating in democracy. But even though Labour has risen from the ashes of low polling through a return to the commonsense populism of building a Britain for the many and not the few, it must remember that we live in uncertain times which makes voters unpredictable. The party must not allow its sudden popularity to blind it; it must be built on more than the temporary whims of the electorate. It's why Labour politicians and supporters must start to come to terms with their failures like Iraq and perhaps their stance on Brexit. They must start telling the hard and bitter truth about how we can build a new and vibrant social democratic state for everyone. They must not develop their policies through polls and triangulations as if human life were an algorithm to be manipulated.

My life has straddled two centuries and I witnessed both great and infamous events, but what defines my personality and how I view Britain and the world stems from my childhood of extreme poverty and those six turbulent years when Labour sought to recreate Britain in the likeness of ordinary people. It's why I have not lost faith in left-wing politics despite my disappointments with many of the leaders who have championed its causes over the decades but were felled by either narcissism or weakness of spirit.

The world we live in today is rife with corruption, populism and economic sectarianism. This is a harbinger of worse things to come. And if we do not fight against austerity, the gradual privatisation of the NHS or our addiction to fake news, we will be frog-marched back to my childhood where no one lived well except the rich.

To Everything There Is a Season

I know my moment on this earth is almost done. I will soon join my mother, my father, sisters, brothers, wife, son and friends who have passed on before me. I have tried to relate to you what I have learned and seen through many years of life because we are in the most dangerous time. It will be up to you to decide whether you fight for sunlight or submit to darkness. I am too old now to do much more but tell the truth about the history of my generation. To survive, live well and enjoy love, you must choose the path of your ancestors. In you is the blood of all those who fought for fair wages, housing, healthcare and defended our island against the tyranny of Hitler. In you is the light that your grandparents had when they fought to preserve and expand the civil society through the welfare state. If you do not call upon the wisdom and the spirit of my generation, you will regress to an era when want and ignorance were as deadly as a pestilence to Britain.

I can't make that decision for you. I have shown you what that world looked like when the 1 per cent enslaved an entire generation to feed their greed. It is now up to you because the sunset has come to my life but you must not let it come to our country. It shouldn't be this way. It should be better for you. You deserve more than the second-rate politics of Theresa May and the third-rate lives many lead because of austerity.

I was born in the darkest of times and it seems because of Brexit and Donald Trump that I will exit this world in a similar era of uncertainty, inequality and cruelty.

Right now, we are at a juncture in history that is as dangerous to this generation as the 1930s were to mine. There are serious threats of war emerging all across the globe, some caused by the folly of neo-liberalism and others just erupting because we forgot that tyranny, if fed, will metastasise in even the healthiest of societies.

It is your choice now to decide whether you let the jungles of greed, neo-liberalism and corporations grow over and obscure the welfare state like vines and forest growth obscured the great Mayan civilisations a millennium ago, or you can reclaim your birth right. My past won't become your future if you hold firm to the belief that all people are born equal and deserve the right to a life free of want, ignorance and sickness. Believe in yourselves, in social justice, and live by the creed that we are all our brother's keeper.

Epilogue

As I write this, it is June 2017 and summer stands before us like an oasis of pleasant diversions from the problems of life in an austere world. But as a heatwave blankets Britain and our beaches are overwhelmed by those in search of a cool tide to wash against their warm feet, the chaos from Brexit, the chaos from terrorism, the chaos from an indecisive election loom on our horizon like a tempest does for a small skiff afloat on a giant ocean.

Whether it's our country's political situation or economic climate, nothing is certain anymore because we now exist on the breath of the Chinese curse to live in interesting times. I have known these unsettled days once before when I was young and lived through a similar crisis of leadership in the 1930s. Then our country and the world hurtled towards a monstrous war. Over seventy-five years on, our civilisation is once again trundling towards something unpleasant unless we make a momentous change to our system of government and economy.

Whatever our destiny is as a nation, there's one sad fact that makes me restless. It's apparent that few of our leaders are up to the task of seeing Britain safely through these treacherous waters. It is a frightening testament of the times we live in that too many of our politicians are not up to their job description. They are woefully unprepared to confront the situations our country must face today. It leaves me beyond despair when I ponder the idea that Boris Johnson is our Foreign Secretary during this epoch of crisis and uncertainty. He is as out of his depth as Donald Trump because his entire CV is a lacklustre list of headline-grabbing follies like the Garden Bridge and water cannons for the London police services. He is the last person you want to rely upon during a crisis, but then so too is everyone in Theresa May's cabinet. They seem made-to-measure for less rigorous pursuits when Britain needs our best minds to ease economic inequalities, calm social divides and negotiate a survivable Brexit.

When I glance at this Tory government's front bench I can plainly see that these politicians came off the rack of a party-political machine that is good at only one thing: promoting opportunists. In their soundbites for the news, Theresa May and her cabinet can come across like a pride of lions, but once they are confronted by the realities of Brexit or terrorism, their roars of defiance are as Shakespeare wrote, 'full of sound and fury, Signifying nothing'.

Epilogue

It's why I felt sickened when Theresa May, after a series of terrorism attacks in London and Manchester in spring 2017, claimed our security had not been compromised by the fact that 20,000 police personnel have been let go during these long years of austerity. Her words sounded as sincere to me as a cheque written on a bankrupt's chequebook, especially since she was compelled to call upon the Army for a short while to assist in anti-terrorist protection. It doesn't take a security expert to deduce that after four major terrorist attacks in three months, which have left scores dead in Manchester and London, that the simple tools of security have been compromised by Tory austerity policies that have gutted our police services.

Terrorism lately has hit our country with the same deadly unexpectedness of the V-2 rocket attacks that I remember from the Second World War. Like then, we are left hesitant and worried for our safety because these attacks are so random, so sudden and so unexpected. As long as the Conservatives insist on doing brisk trade in armaments with the tyrants of the Middle East, I doubt terrorism can be quelled. I was impressed when Labour, during the recent general election, called for a moratorium of arms sales to Saudi Arabia because of their war of aggression in Yemen that has caused an enormous humanitarian crisis.

Terrorism may be an obvious danger to life, but so are many other Tory policies. It is a tragedy of enormous proportions that Britain is led by a Conservative government that is excellent at developing slogans like 'strong and stable' but woefully inadequate in protecting all of its citizens. Ordinary people are under attack from austerity that has left them prey to poverty under a government that has relinquished its responsibilities to provide a safety net of support for all of its citizens. Our health and safety is at risk not just because wages are shrinking and benefits diminishing, but also because the Tories have deregulated many building codes to lessen the costs to landlords. The removal of health and safety regulations can only contribute to greater risk of fire or other calamities that befall tenants.

Over my long life I have been subjected to some atrocious governments. But by far Theresa May's inability to lead, to be resourceful, to be brave, or to be kind has shown her to be the most craven Prime Minister I have yet to encounter. Nothing better amplified her unfitness to govern than her callow response to the Grenfell Tower fire in London in June 2017.

When I first saw Grenfell Tower after the great fire had reduced it to a scorched and desolate building, I was reminded of what the Blitz had done to London's East End over seventy years ago. It saddened and enraged me to see that building, where once life teemed with ordinary concerns, reduced to a burned-out shell. It had been reduced to a hollow husk of anguish, which stretched upwards to the heavens in an indictment to the system below that refused to listen to the safety concerns of the tenants because they were of modest means. In the first week after the tragedy, beneath its charred remains, the residents that survived this terrible, criminal conflagration slept on the floors of churches like refugees from a horrendous war, except all around them was wealth that was indifferent and untouched by their sorrow. This country is angry at the government because all information so far gathered indicates that the enormous loss of life and trauma caused to the survivors can be laid at the feet of Tory austerity. Ordinary people are disturbed by this horrible event because it lays bare the simple truth that their safety is judged to be less important than the bottom line of landlords whose wealth must be preserved at all costs.

Britain's political horizons are overcast because, after decades of neglect, after decades of neo-liberalism, the seasons of discontent approach and we are not prepared. Britain is in a crisis caused by the ineptitude of Theresa May and her failures in policy as well as leadership.

Theresa May's government has stumbled like an antagonistic, drunken wedding guest because it has shown belligerence to the EU and sloppy toadyism to Donald Trump. The Tories have tried to triangulate success and instead ended up antagonising their own base, the left and anyone who desires coherency from government.

On the home front, the carefully structured narrative that Theresa May is the epitome of decisive leadership has come crashing down like a cheap plaster of Paris statue onto a hard floor following the disastrous June 2017 general election. In reckless hubris like Napoleon charging into Russia, Theresa May bet our nation's stability and her legacy on that snap election. Before she rolled the election dice many pundits thought her political legacy would be forged in the steel of a hard Brexit and a right-wing populism that enticed working-class voters to abandon the Labour Party for good. But after reducing her working majority to a hung parliament, Theresa May is now seen as a twenty-first-century Anthony Eden whose vanity, arrogance and sheer stupidity drove Britain into the Suez Crisis of 1956. During the general election, May and her political team acted less like skilled professionals and more like a broken sat-nav instructing the driver to make a right turn off a pier.

Political talk at the beginning of April 2017 was of how the Tories could govern Britain for a generation and that Labour, unless it became a party that favoured more right-wing economic policies under the guise of middle-of-the-road politics, was doomed to obscurity. However, we live in the most unsettled of political times and, because Jeremy Corbyn harnessed the hopes and dreams of the youth vote, Labour was able to get its largest vote share since 2001.

It surprised everyone, including me. Six months ago, when I was first writing the concluding chapters to this book, I was doubtful that Corbyn could survive until autumn 2017. I could not imagine then how our political landscape could change so dramatically. An evening frost had gathered on my living-room window pane while a gas fire kept me warm. The last thing I could have imagined was that when gardens were again ripe with the scent of spring flowers, Theresa May and her Tory government would be hanging onto power by their fingernails because of Jeremy Corbyn and his commonsense revolution.

No, when I sent my manuscript to my publisher, I thought there was nothing more to be said. My history, my hurt, my hopes, my fears and my joys had been drained out of me by writing this book. Emotionally, I'd spent the same force to produce the material for this book as my mother had once used to wring dry my thick corduroy trousers between the grips of two washing rollers. I was empty of memories, having done my best to chronicle the events that have shaped my early life and the problems that beset our country today.

In those cold months of winter, I felt somewhat despondent because Labour then was doing terribly in the polls. My confidence by that time had been tested by Jeremy Corbyn's leadership and I was worried that my support, although sincere, might be as misguided as so many of the paid pundits suggested. It just didn't look like Jeremy Corbyn would ever be permitted to click with the electorate. He was pilloried by both the right-wing and moderate press, and he seemed a man prone to blundering and looking ill-prepared. Prime Minister's Questions at the beginning of the year had become an agony to watch as Corbyn seemed ill-suited to take on the Tories. It was as if he was playing by the Queensberry rules while everyone against him was using knuckle dusters. I was beginning to think Corbyn just didn't have what it took to be a leader. I was beginning to fear that the politics for the many and not the few had been defeated through our support for him. But even though I had these misgivings, I kept them to myself because I didn't believe that attacking Corbyn or his team advanced the cause of social and economic progress. No, all it did was play into the hands of those who are opposed to a fair deal for all Britain's citizens.

I am glad I held my tongue because, even though I still wasn't sure about Jeremy Corbyn's leadership during the first few months of 2017, he showed that there is truth in the saying 'cometh the hour, cometh the man'.

Theresa May and her aids gambled all their political capital on the notion that the people of Britain saw Jeremy Corbyn as unfit to lead Britain. The polls certainly indicated that Corbyn was disliked and not trusted because, at the time when the Prime Minister called her election, Labour was down twenty points. It was predicated that the party could lose between 100 to 200 seats.

At the start of the campaign I remember feeling frustration at Jeremy Corbyn for appearing so blasé when the news showed Labour on its death bed.

Yet the campaign became like the Aesop fable of the race between the tortoise and hare because it turned into a competition of endurance and trust.

Theresa May and her handlers treated the 2017 general election like it was a presidential campaign, which is perhaps why at her first appearance in Bolton, she was brought by helicopter as if she were a populist president in a Latin American nation visiting a secluded jungle outpost. From the start, her election team of cynical operators like the Australian Lynton Crosby or Jim Messina, on loan from the American Democrat Party, hid Theresa May from public scrutiny by keeping her away from the leaders' debate or meeting ordinary voters. Jeremy Corbyn, meanwhile, was seen everywhere by massive, enthusiastic crowds speaking across the country like FDR did to a depression-ravaged United States. Labour on social media changed the Tories' narrative that this election was about Brexit, and made it instead about austerity. It made voters think about the dire economic circumstances in which they had been placed because of Tory mismanagement of the economy and society.

In the north, south and all compass points in Britain, Corbyn delivered speeches of passion and popular eloquence because he talked about wanting a government that was for the many and not the few. I saw him transformed during this election from a fringe politician into a national leader.

Yet it wasn't until Labour produced its election manifesto that I felt Jeremy Corbyn had a real chance of breaking Theresa May's commanding lead in the polls. It was a manifesto that I understood would be a game changer. It held for twenty-first-century voters the same optimism, the same life-changing policies that beguiled me to vote Labour in 1945 at the age of twenty-two.

Corbyn's manifesto wasn't revolutionary: it just contained good and practical policies that would benefit most citizens. It called for things this nation needs, such as the renationalisation of the rail services, as well as an NHS for and by the people. It spoke to the young who have borne the heavy price of austerity by offering free university tuition, a proper housing strategy and a child day-care strategy. Moreover, all of these initiatives by Labour were properly costed, whereas the Tory manifesto called for more austerity, greater personal costs for social care, less taxes for the rich and an end to school meals for the disadvantaged as well as a means-tested winter fuel allowance.

It's no wonder Theresa May's working majority was destroyed by the voters on 8 June 2017. And now, in the wake of her gamble for absolute power in regards to how we exit the EU, Britain has begun Brexit negotiations with a hung parliament in which the Tories must appease the Democratic Unionist Party like an unrequited lover driven to desperation to win the ardour of a disinterested heart. This government is a shambles because Theresa May's greed for power drove her to call an unnecessary election under the pretext that she wanted a strong mandate for a hard Brexit.

With no majority, May and her government have no mandate or any real directive on Brexit from the people. Confidence in the Tory government is as thin and fragile as a shard of ice on a hot day in July. The nation is so unsettled by Theresa May's leadership that, for the first time since the referendum, over half of voters in a recent YouGov poll now want a second referendum.

The PM is a wounded political beast and the cuts she received in the 2017 election are deep enough that in time they will prove to be fatal. The Queen's Speech was bereft of most of the policies outlined in the Tories' election manifesto. Instead, great talk was made of building terminal stations for travel into outer space.

One thing is certain: Theresa May will never be allowed to fight another election by her party. She is a dead woman walking and it is unlikely that she will survive much longer. The only thing that keeps Theresa May as PM is that the Tories have no one who can assume the reins and stop this government galloping out of control. But when she is replaced by another Tory, whether it is Boris Johnson, Andrea Leadsom or another that stalks in the shadows, don't ever believe the Tories if they try to tell you they have changed their stripes. You see, even if the Tories were to end austerity, it can never really be over until they restore all they took away from us in the last seven years and take back all they gave to the wealthy through tax cuts or privatisation of state assets.

So, what remains now in the wake of Theresa May's botched attempt to win glory for herself and greater parliamentary power for the Tories? Without a doubt, we will see another general election very soon and we should accept, owing to the volatility of politics today, that all bets are off. What is essential between now and the next election, if we wish to end austerity and prevent my past becoming your future, is that Labour increases its outreach to the young, the disaffected and the hard-pressed middle class. Labour has a real chance of forming the next government and returning economic and social equality back to this country. To do so will not be easy. It took almost thirty years to destroy the welfare state, and its rebuilding will be a long and arduous task. But, as I saw the foundations dug for a progressive society in 1945, I know we can do it again, although only if we don't succumb to the lure of the Tories and their media, who divide us, cheapen our dignity and make us less civilised.

Acknowledgements

I feel greatly honoured, privileged and quite frankly chuffed to be able to write books in the winter of my years. However, I can't state enough times that the act of writing may be solitary, but the art of making a good book requires the input of many creative people. It's why I have so many people to thank for ensuring that *Don't Let My Past Be Your Future* was able to see the light of day.

First, I must thank my agent Matthew Hamilton who encouraged me and helped place my work into the wonderful and capable hands of Constable. My editors at this wonderful publishing house, Andreas Campomar, Claire Chesser and Howard Watson, ensured that the book you have just read is the best I could offer you. Writing a book that is both political and personal is no easy task, especially when the subject of my early life entails so much tragedy. The professionalism and kindness shown to me by the team at Constable made writing this book a much easier task and for that I will always be grateful to them.

But my greatest thanks must go to my son John who has been by my side since the death of my second son Peter seven years ago. Without John I know that I would not have survived that grief nor would I have had the courage to lay bare the horrors of growing up on the mean streets of Britain during the Great Depression. John is the steady shoulder I can lean on with confidence, knowing that he is not only my son but also my comrade-in-arms.

I must also thank all those who I've crossed paths with during my life because you have made my journey through this world more enjoyable.

Finally, my thanks and appreciation go to all those who have come to hear me speak out against austerity in small and large venues across this country of ours during these last three years. You all give me optimism for the future. I hope that your life will be as long and as healthy as mine. May you all be blessed with the happiness and purpose I was granted.